THE

ARCANA

OF

FREEMASONRY

PLATE G.

The Tableau des Bacabs (restored). The Raised Tatt Cross, with Supporters.

Frontispiece (see p.

THE
ARCANA
OF
FREEMASONRY

ALBERT CHURCHWARD

WEISERBOOKS
Boston, MA/York Beach, ME

This edition first published in 2005 by
Red Wheel/Weiser, LLC
York Beach, ME
With offices at:
368 Congress Street
Boston, MA 02210
www.redwheelweiser.com

Library of Congress Cataloging-in-Publication Data
Churchward, Albert.
 The arcana of freemasonry : a history of Masonic signs and
 symbols / Albert Churchward.
   p. cm.
 ISBN 1-57863-338-9
  1. Freemasonry—History. 2. Freemasonry—Symbolism.
  3. Freemasonry—Rituals. I. Title.
 HS425.C64 2005
 366'.1—dc22

                                          2004061493

Typeset in Adobe Garamond
Printed in Canada
TCP

12 11 10 09 08 07 06 05
 8 7 6 5 4 3 2 1

I dedicate
THIS WORK TO
ALL MY BROTHER MASONS
OF WHATEVER CLIME AND WHATEVER CREED
WHO TAKE AN INTEREST IN
MASONIC RESEARCH

INTRODUCTION
TO THE 2005 EDITION

Albert Churchward was an extraordinary man. After a successful and strenuous career in medicine, this widely travelled and immensely learned man still possessed the energy and enthusiasm to dedicate the second half of his adult life to conducting extensive, detailed research into the origin and development of human society and of the religious impulse in man. This research resulted in six books, published over a period of twenty-five years, in which the origins of human speculative thought were related to the origins and symbolism of Freemasonry.

Such a substantial and apparently magisterial body of work might have been expected to bring Churchward both academic recognition and Masonic honour. As it happened, he received neither. What Churchward *did* receive was scholarly disdain and the ridicule of Masonic historians. And why this came about was perfectly clear. Churchward's rejection by both communities was due to his having committed the cardinal sin of propagating original and controversial ideas that flew in the face of the prevailing orthodoxies of archaeology, anthropology, and Freemasonry.

He placed human origins two million and more years ago in the region of the Great Lakes of East Africa—close enough geographically to the earliest human remains discovered long afterward by Professor Leakey and nowhere near as adventurous in terms of time—but failed to recognize the immense hostility that such Afrocentrism would encounter. He was also astute enough to be sceptical about the nature of the Piltdown skull at a time when many of his contemporaries were happy to accept it as genuine, although scepticism on most other contentious topics was alien to his nature.

As for Freemasonry, Churchward made the startling claim that it (or at least a recognizable forerunner of the Craft) arose among primitive man with the development of what he called the "Stellar

Cult." This belief system was centered, so he claimed, on Polaris and the six other stars in the constellation of Ursa Minor. The people of the Stellar Cult period kept their time by the observation of the recession of the seven Pole stars or Little Bear, which later they named the "Seven Glorious Ones."[1]

But Churchward was at pains to emphasize that these people did not worship the stars, which were simply symbols of divinity: "If a sign or symbol represents the Great God, it is not the sign or symbol they worship, but the *Great God*."[2] Elsewhere he was more specific about the god in question: "The Pole Star was the first fixed point within the Circle, not the Sun, and the earliest Supreme Being, as the head of the seven Primary Stars, was the God of the Pole Star."— Horus.[3]

In itself such claims were well within the realm of what was then considered to be reasonable speculation. The real problem for Churchward was his suggested chronology. The Stellar Cult survived, he insisted, for some 300,000 years after its first appearance about 600,000 years ago. This was enough to astonish the boldest of speculative Masonic historians, but Churchward compounded his rashness by claiming the Great Pyramid of Gizeh belonged to this period. There were many other Masons who believed that the ancient Egyptians were the source of much Masonic symbolism and more than a few who were willing to accept that Egypt had given birth to Freemasonry. But they sensibly balked at such an immense age for the pyramids.

Even Castells—the author of many wildly speculative works on Masonic history and symbolism—objected to this. "Where exactly," he asked Churchward in a letter to *The Freemason*, "can we find any ruined temples of which we may say with any degree of confidence that they are at least 10,000 years old?" Receiving no answer from Churchward, Castells then disputed his dating of Mexican codices and threw in some heavy sarcasm:

1 Albert Churchward, *The Origin and Evolution of Freemasonry: Connected with the Origin and Evolution of the Human Race* (London, 1920), p. 97.
2 Churchward, *The Origin and Evolution of Freemasonry*, p. 115.
3 Churchward, "Point Masonry" in *The Freemason*, November 8, 1913, p. 298.

"The discovery of the American continent took place in A.D. 1502, and it seems to me that the four hundred years that have rolled by since that date cannot count much with one who is dealing with the origin of symbols alleged to be 600,000 years old."[4]

Churchward again ignored the challenge to his dating, but he did take up a spirited defense of his analysis and comparison of ancient symbols. He could not do otherwise, for his theories largely stand or fall by an acceptance or rejection of his interpretation of symbols and his placing of them in a Masonic context. His defense was carried over into his later books, including this one, and as the decipherment of specific religious symbols (as opposed to symbolic alphabets) is a notoriously subjective discipline—Castells commented in the first of his letters that "sign-language is not an exact science"—readers may be left to judge for themselves how successful he was.

Although speculation about Masonic origins and symbolism runs through all of Churchward's books, *The Arcana of Freemasonry* is the only one in which he takes up questions about Freemasonry as we know it, i.e. as it has existed since the founding of the first Grand Lodge in 1717. There is, alas, all too little, for it is on such questions as the future and morality of Masonry that Churchward is, for Masons at least, most stimulating. His principal concern, however, was always the signs, symbols, and practices of Freemasonry, together with their origin and their relationship to the development of the earliest civilizations. And it was over these questions that he faced the most hostile criticism.

In his review of Churchward's *Origin and Antiquity of Freemasonry* (1898), Dr. Westcott of Golden Dawn fame condemned virtually everything about it. He denied a commonality of interpretation between Masonic emblems "and the same emblems found in Egypt, or in India, or elsewhere"; he denied with equal vehemence any

---

4 F. de P. Castells, "Bro. Churchward's Lectures," Letters in *The Freemason*, August 16 and October 18, 1913, pp. 112 and 249.

connection between the Great Pyramid and Speculative Masonry; and he described a similar suggested connection between Masonic rituals and the *Book of the Dead* as "wild fancy."[5] It is probable, however, that Churchward found Westcott's final criticism to be the most telling. Westcott noted, "The volume contains a good many references to the work of Le Plongeon on the archaic remains of Central America, but Le Plongeon is as visionary in his allegorical explanations as the present author."[6]

Churchward refers to Le Plongeon's ideas in *The Arcana* and notes that Le Plongeon and his wife stayed with him as his guests for a considerable time while Le Plongeon was writing his works and that Le Plongeon asked him to read all his manuscripts before they were published. This suggests that in the 1890s Churchward viewed Le Plongeon's ideas sympathetically and thus included them in his first book. But by 1915 he had presumably come to recognize that Westcott's opinion of them was fully justified and so points out with amazing hindsight that even then he had recognized that Le Plongeon's "deductions were, nevertheless, quite erroneous."

But this was an isolated instance. To the end of his life Churchward stoutly maintained the truth of his views about human and Masonic origins, despite continuing opposition and hostility. The antagonism was not universal, however, for when he died the obituaries in the Masonic press were affectionate tributes to Churchward as a man and a Mason. But they tell us little about his life.

What is known is that Albert Churchward was born on September 3, 1852, although it is not recorded where, and died in London on September 4, 1925. Churchward's medical career began at Guy's Hospital in London and led to his qualifying as M.R.C.S. in 1874. Two years later he obtained his M.R.C.P. at Edinburgh and his doctorate in medicine at the University of Brussels. He then travelled extensively, especially around southern Africa. But medical practice was not the whole of his working life. Churchward was also an inventor, producing a "hygienic bicycle saddle,"—there is, alas, no

5 W. Wynn Westcott, "Review of *Origin and Antiquity of Freemasonry* by Albert Churchward," in *Ars Quatuor Coronatorum*, vol. 12, 1899, p. 40.
6 loc. cit.

picture of it—improved cycle pedals, and a new process of hardening steel and armour plates.

His Masonic career began when he was a young man. In 1878 he was initiated into the Hornsey Lodge in London; later, he became Master of the Lodge and entered its associated Royal Arch Chapter. Outside these basic degrees he became a member of the Ancient & Accepted Rite (the English version of what is known in America as the Scottish Rite), eventually presiding over the Alleyn Chapter as its "Most Wise Sovereign." There would be nothing unusual about this except that in England the Ancient & Accepted Rite is a wholly Christian degree and requires its members to hold a Christian Trinitarian faith. Whatever Churchward's true beliefs may have been, not even his most ardent apologist could possibly present him as an orthodox Christian.

Even a cursory reading of *The Arcana*—or of any of his other books—shows quite clearly that Churchward saw Christ as a symbolic and not a historic figure. In "Symbols of Egyptian Concepts," an article written for *The Freemason*,[7] Churchward draws an exact parallel between Christian and Egyptian beliefs and identifies Horus with Christ. He had done much the same in *Signs and Symbols of Primordial Man* (1908) and hinted at it in his first book *Origin and Antiquity of Freemasonry*. Then Westcott, who was offended that a fellow member of a Christian degree should remain in it under what he saw as false pretences, took him to task:

> I yet do not see that much light is thrown by the
> Book of the Dead upon that very High Church
> Christian degree [the 18° of the Ancient &
> Accepted Rite], the ritual of which has no trace
> of any purely Egyptian symbolism, the only allu-
> sions to names and places found in it being taken
> from the New Testament.[8]

At the time Churchward made no response, but in 1920 he set out his analysis of the Egyptian origin of the various degrees of the

7 *The Freemason*, September 27, 1913, p. 204.
8 loc. cit.

Ancient & Accepted Rite and provided what he claimed were the true names that should be used in the rituals of those degrees.[9] What the Supreme Council, who had charge over the Ancient & Accepted Rite, thought of his suggestions is not recorded, but it does seem likely that part of the hostility to Churchward and his ideas in English Masonic circles was the result of his rejection of Christian orthodoxy.

There is no question, however, that Churchward believed in God. He viewed the evolution of religion as a progression from primitive Totemism, through a symbolic belief system, to a philosophical understanding of one God—presented in ideal form within Freemasonry as the Great Architect of the Universe. For him Freemasonry is a paradigm of human progress, social structure, and spirituality. Because religion and politics, in their denominational or party sense, are excluded from Masonic activities, Masons, he believed, "possess the dominant power for the advancement and good of humanity generally" and are thus ideally placed to be the leaders of society. But only if they begin to practice what they preach, and Churchward was well aware that the Craft is far from perfect.

The perfect society that he wished to see would not, however, be recognized as such by most of us. Churchward was inevitably a child of his times: he was elitist, chauvinistic, and racist. He can be forgiven for his expressed hostility to German Masonry—the First World War was raging when *The Arcana* was published—and his pathological fear and hatred of Socialism was not uncommon within the professional classes, but his views on racial evolution are both archaic and unpleasant. His later books, in which he expounds at length his notion of the development of the human race as a linear progression from the Pigmy to the White Man, also recycled a number of his scientific essays. These present an eccentric theory of "corpuscles," which correspond more or less to electrons and are seen as the basis not only of organic and inorganic matter, but also of the spiritual essence that energizes the former. Added to all this is a very inaccurate and outdated cosmology, and it is perhaps as

9 Churchward, *The Origin and Evolution of Freemasonry*, pp. 179-189.

well that the books that followed *The Arcana* have faded into oblivion.

Is there, then, a real justification for reissuing *The Arcana of Freemasonry*? There is, because Churchward, in spite of his eccentricities, raised serious questions about the purpose and function of Freemasonry in modern society that still require answers from those who lead the Craft today. More than this, his work on symbols does have merit; there is more to their study than historical analysis. The anonymous reviewer in *The Freemason*, supporting Churchward, believed that Egyptian symbols point out

> the relationship between matter and consciousness, the initiate and the Supreme. The symbol always becomes overshadowed by the powerful thoughts which it calls forth—thoughts for which no language is provided, but which come forth unbidden whenever the symbol appears.[10]

If his work provides a signpost for the psycho-spiritual study of symbolism, then we indeed owe a debt to Albert Churchward.

—R.A. Gilbert,
Bristol, England, March 2004

---

10 "The Arcana of Freemasonry," unsigned review in *The Freemason*, September 18, 1915, p. 166.

CONTENTS

VII

PRINCIPAL ILLUSTRATIONS

And numerous Figures and Diagrams in the Text.

The Arcana of Freemasonry

I

FREEMASONRY—THE BRIDGE OF HIS-TORY—UNITING THE PAST WITH THE PRESENT

I.—DIFFERENT OPINIONS AS REGARDS THE ORIGIN OF FREEMASONRY AND A MODERN INTRODUCTION IN VARIOUS COUNTRIES.

"Egypt! how I have dwelt with you in dreams
So long, so intimately, that it seems
As if you had borne me: Though I could not know
It was so many thousand years ago!
And in my gropings darkly underground,
The long-lost memory at last is found
Of Motherhood—you the Mother of us all!
And to my fellow-men I must recall
The memory too : that common Motherhood
May help to make the common brotherhood."

GERALD MASSEY.

THE origin of Freemasonry is one of the most interesting subjects to which the Masonic student can apply his time and talent.

There are authors who attribute the origin of modern Freemasonry to the followers of Pythagoras, because some of the speculations of that philosopher concerning the meaning of numbers are to be found in the esoteric doctrines taught in Masonic Lodges. Others, on account of the Christian symbols that have been incorporated in the decorating of things pertaining to Masonry, follow the Swedish system, and say that the Essenes and the first Christians founded it. Others, again, make it originate in the building of Solomon's Temple; many Jewish names, emblems, and legends, taken from the V.S.L., having found their way into the rites of Initiation and in several degrees. And still others state that it goes back to Adam; ask why—they do not know. Thomas Payne and those of his school say that the Druids were the fathers of the Craft, they being *supposed* worshippers of the sun, moon, and stars, these jewels of the firmament being represented on the ceilings of the Masonic Temples.

Dance of Villoison speaks of Herculanæum as its birthplace, because of the many similarities that existed between the Collegia of the Romans and the Lodges of the operative Masons of the Middle Ages.

Michael Andrew Ramsey, a Scotch gentleman, in a discourse delivered in Paris, in 1740, suggested the possibility of the fraternity having its origin in the time of the Crusades among the Knights Templar, and explains it in this way: The Pope, Clement V, and Philippe le Bel, King of France, fearing the power of the Templars and coveting their immense wealth, resolved to destroy the Order. When, in 1308, Jacques de Molay, then Grand Master of the Order, was preparing an expedition to avenge the wrongs and disasters suffered by the Christians in the East, the Pope, the only Sovereign Power to which, in the spiritual, the Templars owed allegiance, enticed him to France. On his arrival he was received with every mark of friendship; but soon after the King caused him to be arrested, together with some other dignitaries, accusing them of the most heinous crimes, imputing to them the secret rites of their initiation. By order of the Archbishop of Sens and his provincial council, Jacques de Molay, Guy of Auvergne, and several other officers were burned alive on 18th March, 1314. The Pope, by a Bull, dated the 2nd of April, and published on the 2nd of May, 1312, that he issued on his own responsibility —the Council of Vienne, in Dauphiné, being adverse to hasty measures—declared the Order abolished throughout the world. The execution of the Grand Master and his companions gave the "coup de grâce" to the Order, but some of the Knights who had escaped to Portugal continued the Order. They assumed the title of Knights of Christ, which the order still bears. Jacques de Molay, before his death, had appointed Johan Marcus Larmenio as his successor to the office of Grand Master. The Knights who, fleeing from the persecution, had taken refuge in Scotland at the Court of King Robert Bruce, refused to recognize his authority ; and pretending to re-establish the Order of the Temple, under the allegory and title of Architects, protected by the King, laid the foundation of the Order of Free and Accepted Masons of the Scottish Rite, in 1314. The new society soon forgot the meaning of the execratory oath that the members were obliged to take at their initiation ; the death of Clement V, of Philippe le Bel, of the accusers and enemies of Jacques de Molay, and the other Knights who had been executed, having removed the object of their vengeance. Still they continued to decorate their Lodges with tokens commemorative of the death of the Grand Master, and to impose on all new members the obligation of avenging it, which they signified by striking with an unsheathed dagger at unseen beings, his supposed murderers. This allegory is well known to the Knights of Kadosh. A century had scarcely elapsed when this idea was abandoned—the founders and their disciples having passed away, their successors saw only allegories in the Symbols of the Order—and the extensive use

of words and texts taken from the Bible was introduced. The enemies of Cromwell and of the
Republic, having in view the re-establishment of
the monarchy, created the Degree of Grand Master
to prepare the minds of the masses for that event.
King William III was initiated.

Masonry, says Preston, was very much neglected
as early as the reign of James II, and even after
this period it made but slow progress until 1714,
when King George I ascended the throne. Three
years later, in February, 1717, the first Grand
Lodge was established in London. A committee
from the four Lodges then existing in that city
met at the tavern of the "Apple Tree," and
nominated Anthony Sayer, who was elected Grand
Master on the 24th of the following June, the day
of St. John the Baptist, and for that reason St.
John was selected as the patron of the Order.

This origin of the Craft is credited by many
authorities on the subject. They found their
opinion on the fact that many of the ceremonies
practised by the "Architects" are still observed
among Masons, and that the Grand Lodge preserved the fundamental laws, together with the
spirit of the ancient Brotherhood. Others, who
claim to be well informed, are of opinion that it
did not originate in any Order of Chivalry, but
the building fraternities of the Middle Ages.

From 1738, however, Lodges sprang up over

Europe at a rapid rate, notwithstanding the bitter opposition of the Church of Rome, which fulminated against it in most terrible anathemas, as early as 1738, at the instigation of the Inquisition. Pope Clement XII, on the 28th of April of that year, caused a prohibitory Bull to be issued against Freemasons, entitled " In Eminenti," in which he excommunicated all Masons ; and the Cardinal Vicar of Rome, by edict, in the name of the High Priest of the God of Peace and Mercy, decreed the penalty of death against them in 1739 ; and in May, 1751, Pope Benoit XIV renewed the Bull of Clement XII by another, beginning with these words : " Providas Romanorum Pontificum."

Lodges were established in France in 1725, and on the 14th September, 1732, all Masonic Associations were prohibited by the Chamber of Police of the Châtelet of Paris.

In 1727 Lord Coleraine founded a Lodge in Gibraltar, and in the succeeding year in Madrid, the capital of Spain, the stronghold of the Inquisition.

In 1740, in consequence of the Bull of Clement XII, King Philip V of Spain promulgated an order against Masons in his kingdom, many of whom were arrested and sent to the galleys. The Inquisitors took advantage of the opportunity to persecute the members of the Lodge they discovered in Madrid. They caused them to be loaded with chains, to be obliged to row in the galleys, with a scanty supply of food of the poorest quality, but plenty of bastinado. King Fernando VI renewed the ordinance on 2nd July, 1751, making Masonry high treason.

In 1735 a Lodge was established at Lisbon, the capital of Portugal, by some of the descendants of the Knights Templar who fled there, under the title of "Knights of Christ." These have kept alive the ancient Order in defiance of the Pope's Bulls.

In 1730 a great many Germans were initiated in England. In 1733 the Grand Master, Lord Strathmore, authorized eleven of the Brotherhood to open the Hamburg Lodge. In 1740 B. Puttman, of the Hamburg Lodge, received a Patent of Provincial Grand Master from England, and the Lodge assumed the title of Absalom. King Frederick II, who had been initiated when Crown Prince of Prussia, continued to give support, and assumed the title of "Grand Master Universal, and Conservator of the Most Ancient and Most Respectable Association of Ancient Freemasons or Architects of Scotland." He cemented together again the Order which had become scattered, so far as he was able, and signed the Constitution in his Palace, at Berlin, 1st May, 1786, saving Freemasonry from annihilation in Germany.

In 1732 we find the first Lodge in America ; it was held in the " Tun Tavern " in Philadelphia, the brethren having previously met in Boston, which may be regarded as the birthplace of American Freemasonry. Henry Price was the first Provincial Grand Master appointed by the Grand Lodge of England on 30th April, 1733.

It was established in Italy in the same year.

In 1735 the Grand Duke Francis of Lorraine was initiated. He protected the Masons, and the Craft flourished in Italy until 1737, when Juan Gascon of Medicis, Grand Duke of Tuscany, issued a decree of prohibition against it. Soon after his death, which occurred the same year, the Lodges which had been closed were reopened. It was not long, however, before they were denounced to Pope Clement XII, who issued his Bull of 28th April, 1738, and sent an inquisitor to Florence, who caused various members of the Society to be cast into dungeons. They were set at liberty as soon as Francis of Lorraine became Grand Duke of Tuscany. He not only protected the Masons, but founded lodges in Florence and other places on his estates.

G. Findel was a great advocate that Free-masonry was not derived from the mysteries of the ancients ; he says : " Seeing that the ancient symbolical marks and ceremonies in the Lodges bear very striking resemblance to those of the

mysteries of the ancients, some have allowed themselves to be deceived, and led others astray,
imagining they can trace back the history of the
Craft into the cloudy mist of antiquity ; instead
of endeavouring to ascertain how and when these
ceremonies were introduced into our present system,
they have taken it for granted that they were
derived from the religious mysteries of the
ancients."

Now I propose to trace these mysteries, for the
information of the Brotherhood throughout the
world.

"The cloudy mists of antiquity " may no longer
remain ; within the past few years we have discovered how to decipher and read the ancient
writings on the walls of old ruined temples and
cities in Africa, Asia, and North, Central, and
South America, as well as the ancient writings on
papyri, and these give the key to unlock the
mysteries of the past and reveal the origin of our
Signs, Symbols, and Rituals ; and these I trace
back to Ancient Egypt, and in no other part of the
world can the origins be found.

If we take the theory propounded by Krause,
what do we find? He has endeavoured to prove
that Freemasonry "originated " in the association
of operative Masons, who, in the Middle Ages,
travelled through Europe, and by whom the
Cathedrals and Monasteries were built. But the

secrets these operative Masons had were received from the Chaldean Magicians. These Chaldean or Turanian Priests were the working or operative Masons of the old Egyptian Stellar Mythos Cult, from the seventeenth Nome of Upper Egypt, and were styled Companions (see Ritual).[1] They were initiated in the first and second degree only of the old Egyptian Cult, because they, and they, alone, were employed to look after the building of the Temples and keep the secrets of the same.

These Turanians, who were called "Companions" in Egyptian, only knew the secrets of two of the degrees out of the Seven Primary Mysteries, which were Astro-Mythological. We ordinary Masons, M.M. and up to P.Z., only have these Seven Mysteries. The Greater Mysteries belonging to the Egyptian Eschatology were ten in number.

If we trace these old Turanians (operatives) back to Egypt, we find them well established at the commencement of the Stellar Cult—but it is possible to trace them farther back than this, even to Early Totemic Sociology.

In Africa, at the present day, there exist some of the Nilotic Negroes, descendants of those who first formed the "Nomes" in Egypt ; those who formed the seventeenth Nome are now " the Elgunono."

---

[1] By the word " Ritual " used I allude to the Ritual of Ancient Egypt, the so-called Book of the Dead.

These tribes still, at the present time, are mostly formed into a "secret brotherhood," and by some are called the Blacksmiths. "Horus-Behutet," the first worker in metals, is their chief or head Deity ; our word T.C. is thus a substituted word. Their chief priest is called Ol-Aibon, and they still have many of the primary Symbols and Signs we use. These, with the Madi ,(who were the first builders) and Masai, ultimately all settled in Egypt and formed the early Stellar Mythos people. An early exodus from these tribes, to other parts of the world, was made by the old Turanians.

The Stellar Cult existed for at least three hundred thousand years, as witnessed by records found and still extant. These people travelled and went out over Europe, Asia, part of North and South America, Central America, and the Islands of the Pacific, as well as Africa. The remains and ruins of the large cities and Temples found throughout the world were mostly built by these people. The Solar, who came after, built some, but the buildings of each are easily distinguished one from the other. The former were iconographic, the latter were not. They worked out all the revolutions of the Sun, Moon, and Stars, and the Ritual of Ancient Egypt upon which all doctrines throughout the world have been founded. So that for the oldest records of our Brotherhood we have to go back as far as Totemic Sociology over six hundred thousand years. This is proved by the fact that skeletons of Stellar Mythos people were found in Lombardy in the Pliocene strata—and the above is a low estimate for that.

Now we find from these old Temples that all our Signs and Symbols were in use then just as we use them now ; there is no difference, except that in some cases we have slightly modernised them. Their Rituals, with slight modifications, were the same as ours.

Here we see Krause's theory not without some semblance of plausibility, as Rome, during several centuries, held sway over Gaul and Britain. Roman colonists settled in various parts of these countries, and with their language and customs they imported many of their institutions and associations. That of the Builders, or Collegia, held their Lodges wherever they established themselves, and no doubt initiated new members, and as these countries freed themselves from the yoke of Rome the associations would still remain. But they at best were only carriers of the " operative masons "—Egypt was their birthplace, and we can identify the Nome as the seventeenth Nome from the Ritual, these names, for instance, " Companions "—carried out of Egypt by the Turanians, who spread over Europe ; Asia, except the North ; lower part of North America, Central America, South America, as far down as Chili, in the

Caroline Islands of the Pacific—but not in North Asia, Australia, Tasmania, or extreme North America.

Chevalier Ramsay stated that modern Masonry had its beginning in the Society of Architects founded in Scotland under the protection of King Robert Bruce, and the title of " Ancient and Accepted Masons of the Scottish Rite " may possibly have been formed in Scotland there and then ; but, if that is so, we must trace the origin of this to the Order of Knights Templar, who fled to Scotland, and through them to the Ancient Mysteries practised in the East. From whence did these Templars obtain them? It is well known that one of the charges made against Jacques de Molay and his associates by their accusers was that " they used sacred rites in their initiations." Their four oaths are well known, but who knew their rites of initiation? The aim of the Society of Architects was to perpetuate the ancient Order of the Temple, and they continued to use their initiations of members, symbols, signs, and some parts of the initiatory rites, which had been obtained in the East, but they only knew three degrees out of the seven lesser and ten greater. The next question is : From whence did the Templars receive those symbols, and their esoteric meaning, in which we plainly trace the doctrines of the old Egyptians? No doubt from the Christians, who, like the

Emperor Julian, the Bishop of Synnesius, Clement of Alexandria, and many other philosophers, had been initiated into some of the mysteries by the Priests of Egypt before being converted to Christianity. In this way may be traced how part of the religious mysteries of Egypt, signs and symbols, etc., came to Scotland.

We must remember that the mysteries practised by the Samothracia, Greeks, Romans, Pythagoreans, the mysteries of Eleusis, the mysteries established by Zoroaster, and the Mahatmas, or Brothers of India, all took their origin from the Egyptian Eschatology. We see also from the above how, in one way, the so-called Higher Degrees (The Ten Greater Mysteries) were introduced here in Britain.

The reluctance of the Egyptians to admit strangers to the holy secret of their mysteries was for a very long time insuperable. They, however, at intervals, admitted to the first and second degrees personages noted for their wisdom and knowledge. They admitted the great philosopher Thales, who went to Egypt to learn Geometry and Astronomy about 587 B.C., and Zoroaster 5000 B.C. Another was Eumolpus, King of Eleusis, who, on returning to his country, instituted the mysteries of that name, which he had learnt from the Priests of Egypt. Orpheus, the Greek poet, was also initiated into the first degree. Pythagoras was initiated, but had not the courage to go through to the third degree, only the first and second. The Pelasgians had initiated to the first and second degrees the Samothracia. These Pelasgians obtained their knowledge from the Egyptian Priests direct.

As regards the origin from the Druids. I have given in " Signs and Symbols of Primordial Man " the proofs of the origin of the Druids, and where they came from. They were High Priests of Egypt, who left the mother country at the early part of the Solar Cult, and were therefore well versed both in the seven Lesser Mysteries and the ten Greater Mysteries ; and these practised their religious rites in England until the edict of Canute prohibited their open worship. Canute reigned from 1015 to 1036. To evade persecution they resorted to private meetings and secret celebrations. I do not entertain any doubt that they formed the first so-called "Lodges" in England, as a cloak to screen their religious rites and ceremonies, and to keep them as pure as they had received them originally from their parent sources in Egypt. Many of these old Druid Priests joined the Christian Church, and were the so-called Culdees, but although they had joined the Christian Church they kept themselves very much aloof for a long period, up to the twelfth century.

These were the last remnants of the old Druid
Priests—descendants of their Egyptian brethren—
who practised the pure Eschatology of their forefathers. Gradually they all died out as a separate
and distinct class, and those who remained were
merged into Christianity ; but up to the twelfth
century at least they brought all their doctrines
with them, and practised them in secret places, in
so-called Lodges.

Here we have one source of the origin of Freemasonry, both in the Lesser Mysteries (seven
Degrees) and in the ten Greater Mysteries—so-
called Higher Degrees in this country.

The Druids, in Gaul, were mostly put to the
sword, others fled to this country for protection,
when the Roman Christian doctrines were brought
to them. In America it was the same. As soon
as the Spanish Roman Priests arrived there they
persecuted all the Solar and Stellar people, mur-
dered their priests, overthrew their Temples, and
scattered them with fire and sword. Yet there is
sufficient evidence left in their Signs, Symbols, and
writings on the wall which prove my contention
that all these had the same Eschatology, signs,
symbols, and rites as the Old Egyptians, from
whence they came, and that all these are analogous
to our own with really very little innovation, considering the many thousands of years that these
have been handed down from country to country,

and generation to generation, as we must acknowledge to have been the case if we study the
history of the human past.

There were also many who crossed over to
Europe from Egypt, and spread from Italy into
France, who possessed and clung to the true
doctrines, endured torture, and some even death, by
the early Roman Priests, who tried to usurp the
temporal power by destroying the spiritual ideas ;
and yet these brothers would rather suffer death
than give up their secrets and beliefs. Many of
these migrations can be traced through Europe
and finally to Scotland.

We must also remember that from the downfall of the old Egyptian Empire, up to within
the last few hundred years, we have possessed
no readable records of the past history of mankind. Our History of the World is quite recent,
all the rest is tradition only. Therefore, if you
do not read the Hieroglyphics and Glyphs, " The
Writings on the Wall," you still remain in ignorance
of the history of the human race, and of the origin
and antiquity of Freemasonry. There were no
records left otherwise than these. But these
records have been left for the future student to
decipher and translate. What records will be left
in these islands after another twenty thousand
years have passed, or less?

Again, is it reasonable to suppose that the huge

continents of North and South America have lain unknown by the great communities of Europe, Asia, and Africa until the yesterday of Columbus ; unknown throughout the ages of the vast time that man has existed? Columbus reached America less than five centuries ago, and Eric the Red and his early Norsemen in 983. *The Chinese have written records of trading with America in 500 B.C., and of sending some of their Buddhist Priests there, who returned with the news that they had met Priests with religious writings, signs, and symbols similar to their own,* which, you may see by my "Origin and Evolution of the Human Race," had been established in America at least three hundred thousand years before. Let me also state here that there is no question of "having one's faith shaken." What I write and state for all my Brothers throughout the world is *The Truth. That is what you want to know; that is what you are all striving to obtain,* and if you follow the evolution of the human race in all its phases, you will obtain it, but not otherwise.

I am much indebted to Brother Ham-Smith, P.G.D. Surrey, for the following. It is quite interesting, but I do not vouch for the facts having occurred at the dates as here stated. It is worth recording, however, and research should be made to discover the truth if possible :—

" *The History and Antiquities of the Borough and
Town of Weymouth and Melcombe Regis.*"
By George Alfred Ellis, Surgeon, etc. 1829.

PAGE 4 : " The earliest evidence there is of
this town is about nine hundred years ago, where
the Saxon Chronicles state that King Athelstan,
A.D. 938, in consequence of a false charge being
brought against his half-brother Prince Edwin [1]
of a conspiracy to dethrone him, ordered him to
be exposed in an open boat without sails or oars
to the fury of the raging waves."

PAGE 5 : " In the year 980 Dunstan [Arch-
bishop of Canterbury] was Grand Master of the
fraternity of free and accepted Masons in
England."

PAGE 33 : " Ralph of Monthermer [who was
married to the widow of Gilbert De Clare, Earl
of Hertford and Gloucester, temp. Edward I] was
raised to the degree of Grand Master of the beautiful and sublime mysteries of freemasonry in all
England at the death of Gilbert De Clare, 1280."

[1] Prince Edwin, it appears, had visited the East, and while
there, had been initiated into the sublime mysteries of Freemasonry ; on his return, he instituted a grand lodge at York,
was elected Grand Master of the Craft in England, and formed
the constitution of the English Lodges. It is more than probable
that the necessary meetings of the Craft, whose sublime mysteries
are excluded from the profane eyes of the *communis vulgus*,
were the cause of this suspicion of his conspiring against the
throne of his brother and led to his murder.

The following extracts from an historical record of the successful efforts made for the Union of the Grand Lodges and the final establishment of the United Grand Lodge of England in 1813 is reprinted from *The Freemason* of 27th December, 1913, and will be of interest to readers of the foregoing :—

St. John's Day in winter—the 27th December —has always been recognized as the great Festival of the Order of Freemasons. It was on this day, a hundred years ago, that the Union of the several Grand Lodges in England was consummated.

GRAND LODGES OF ENGLAND.

Formerly England had four Grand Lodges. The oldest, and much the strongest, was founded at the Apple Tree Tavern, Charles Street, Covent Garden, London, in 1717. Members of it traced their origin to an assemblage of Freemasons by King Athelstan at York, in A.D. 926. The Scotch Lodges did not go back nearly so far. They were content to claim descent from those foreign Masons who came to their country in the twelfth century to build the abbeys of Melrose, Holyrood, and Kilwinning, and there is abundant evidence that the Lodges of York and Kilwinning were the parents of many Lodges founded in various parts of Great Britain. The Brethren of York, conscious that their city was the Mecca of Freemasonry, and believing that their Time Immemorial Lodge was a direct descendant of that which was existing in the fourteenth century, determined that they would not be behind those of London, and in 1725 formed the Grand Lodge of All England. Despite its ambitious title, it had a very chequered career down to the last decade of the eighteenth century. About 1740 it, as did also the private York Lodge, became dormant. Both were revived in 1761, but there is no evidence of their existence after 1792. That Grand Lodge confined its activities within a limited area of " All England." Under its banner were two Lodges in the City of York, one each in Scarborough, Ripon, Knaresborough, Hovingham, Swainton, and Rotherham, in Yorkshire ; one in Macclesfield, Cheshire ; and one in Hollingwood, Lancashire. The Grand Lodge of All England also chartered at York the Grand Lodge of England south of the River Trent in 1779. It consisted of discontented members of the Time Immemorial Lodge of Antiquity, of the Premier Grand Lodge (of which Sir Christopher Wren in its day was the Grand Master), and it granted warrants to only two Lodges, both in London. One was named Perfect Observance, the other Perseverance and Triumph. The career of this

" Mushroom Grand Lodge," as the late Bro. W. J. Hughan described it, was as inglorious as that of its parent.

FORMIDABLE RIVAL

The fourth Grand Lodge was the only real rival of the Premier Grand Lodge. It was constituted on July 17th, 1751, at the Turk's Head Tavern, Greek Street, Soho, London, as " The Grand Lodge of England, according to the Old Institutions." Its members were designated " Ancients," while those of the body from which it had seceded were known as " Moderns." The " Ancients " were also spoken of as " Athol Masons," they having elected the third Duke of Athol as their first Grand Master in 1772, his son succeeding to the office at his death.   Two reasons are offered for the founding of the new Grand Lodge.   One is that the Regular Grand Lodge adopted severe measures against recalcitrant and impecunious Lodges. The other is that it introduced innovations in the customs of the Craft which were particularly objected to by the operative section.   " The new body," wrote the late Bro. W. J. Hughan in his introduction to the monumental work of his friend, the late Bro. John Lane, " Masonic Records, 1717-1894," " became very popular, and in a few years was no mean competitor ; its prototype and senior, but less pretentious organization, having also to contend against the introduction of the ' Royal Arch,' which was warmly supported, though not originated, by the ' Ancients,' who became known as the Grand Lodge of ' Four Degrees,' thus (for a time only) placing the parent society at a disadvantage."

BLAST AND COUNTER-BLAST

The " Ancients " having established many Lodges and Provincial Lodges in England and in foreign countries, particularly in America, and having obtained the recognition of the Grand Lodges of Ireland and Scotland, and the almost unanimous support of the Grand Lodges of America, were eager to maintain their independence, and rejected all overtures tendered by the " Moderns " for reunion ; and in 1757 unanimously ordered :—

> That if any Master, Wardens, or presiding officer, or any other person whose business it may be to admit members or visitors, shall admit or entertain in his or their Lodge during Lodge hours, or the time of transacting the proper business of Freemasonry, any Brother or visitor not strictly an Ancient Mason conformable to the Grand Lodge rules and order,

such Lodge so transgressing shall forfeit its
warrant, and the same may be disposed of
by Grand Lodge.

In 1801 the older Grand Lodge issued a counter-
blast. Some of its members were convicted of
having patronized and acted as principal officers
in " an irregular society calling themselves Ancient
Masons, in open violation of the laws of the Grand
Lodge " ; and it was determined that the laws
should be enforced against these offending
Brethren, unless they immediately abandoned
such irregular meetings. These Brethren solicited
the indulgence of the Grand Lodge for three
months, hoping that during the interval they might
be able to effect a union between the two
societies. The indulgence was granted, and " that
no impediment might pervert so desirable an
object, the charge against the offending Brethren
was withdrawn, and a committee, consisting of
Lord Moira and several other eminent characters,
was appointed to pave the way for the intended
union, and every means ordered to be used to
bring the erring Brethren to a sense of their duty
and allegiance." Nothing came of this, for two
years later the Grand Lodge was informed " that
the irregular Masons still continued refractory, and
that so far from soliciting readmission among the
Craft, they had not taken any steps to effect a

union." Their conduct was deemed highly censurable, and the laws of the Grand Lodge were ordered to be enforced against them. It was also unanimously resolved :—

> That whenever it shall appear that any Masons under the English Constitution shall in future attend, or countenance any Lodge or meeting of persons calling themselves Ancient Masons, under the sanction of any person claiming the title of Grand Master of England, who shall not have been duly elected in the Grand Lodge, the laws of the society shall not only be strictly enforced against them, but their names shall be erased from the list, and transmitted to all the regular Lodges under the Constitution of England.

LORD MOIRA'S EFFORTS

In 1806 Lord Moira reported to Grand Lodge that he had visited the Grand Lodge of Scotland and explained the position relating to the " Modern " and " Ancient " Masons in England, and that the Scottish Brethren had declared that they had been always led to think that the " Moderns " were of very recent date and of no magnitude, and being convinced of their error were

desirous that the strictest union should subsist
between the Grand Lodge of England and Scotland, and in proof thereof elected the Prince of
Wales Grand Master of Scotland.   Lord Moira
further stated that when the Scottish Brethren expressed a hope that the differences between the
English Masons would be speedily settled, he
replied that after the rejection of the propositions
of the Grand Lodge by the " Ancients " three
years before, it could not now, consistently with
its honour, make any further advances, but would
always be open to accept the mediation of the
Grand Lodge of Scotland if it should think proper
to interfere.   Two years afterwards the Grand
Lodge of Ireland approved the declaration of their
Scottish Brethren, and pledged itself " not to
countenance or receive as a Brother any person
standing under the interdict of the Grand Lodge
of England for Masonic transgression."   In April,
1809, the Grand Lodge agreed in opinion with
the Committee of Charity that " it is not necessary any longer for to continue in force those
measures which were resorted to in or about the
year 1789 respecting irregular Masons, and do
therefore enjoin the several Lodges to revert to
the ancient landmarks of the Society."   This was
accepted as a step towards the much desired union.
Still, more than four years elapsed before it was
achieved ; and then it came about as the result

of the tactful intervention of three of the sons of George III. The Prince of Wales, who was initiated in 1787 at the Star and Garter Tavern, in Pall Mall, became Grand Master of the Premier Grand Lodge of England in 1790. When he accepted the Regency he vacated the office, and his Brother,

THE DUKE OF SUSSEX,

was elected to succeed him. The venerable and worthy head of the " Ancients," the Duke of Athol, was, says a contemporary record, " soon convinced by the Royal Duke's arguments, strengthened by his own good sense and benevolent mind, how desirable must be an actual and cordial relation of the two societies under one head ; for, to pave the way for the Masons, his Grace, in the handsomest measure, resigned his seat of Grand Master." He recommended as his successor the Duke of Kent, father of Queen Victoria, he having been initiated under the " Ancient " constitution in the Union Lodge of Geneva. The Duke of Kent was acclaimed Grand Master in 1813. The two Royal Dukes, taking into counsel three distinguished Brethren belonging to each society, arranged Articles of Union between the two Grand Lodges of England, and these were ratified, confirmed, and sealed in each of those Lodges on 1st December, 1813.

The same day a joint meeting of the Grand
Lodges received the articles " with Masonic accla-
mation," and to carry them into effect constituted
a Lodge of Reconciliation, consisting of equal
members of the Old Institutions and the Constitution of England. Every care was taken that the
parties to the union should be on a level of
equality. As to the precedence of the Lodges,
it was arranged that the two first Lodges under
each Grand Lodge should draw lots for priority.
The draw favoured the " Ancients," whose Grand
Masters' Lodge became No. 1 on the revised roll,
the Lodge of Antiquity of the Regular Grand
Lodge taking the second position, No. 2 of the
" Ancients " in the same order taking No. 3, and
the second of the Time-Immemorial Lodges
becoming No. 4. " For two such old Lodges
to accept lower positions in the united roll than
their age entitled them to says much," wrote Bro.
Hughan, " for the truly Masonic spirit of their
members, who, to promote peace and harmony,
consented to their juniors taking precedence of
Lodges in existence prior to the formation of the
Premier Grand Lodge." Up to the time of the
union " Modern " Lodges placed on the roll
numbered 1,085, while " Ancient " Lodges war-
ranted between 1751 and 1813 were 521. The
reunion of the two Grand Lodges of England was
consummated with great solemnity on

ST. JOHN'S DAY, 27TH DECEMBER, 1813,

in the Freemasons' Hall, London. The platform
on the east was reserved for the Grand Masters,
Grand Officers, and visitors. Masters, Wardens,
and Past Masters, all dressed in black (except
regimentals), with their respective insignia, and
with white gloves, occupied the sides of the hall,
the Masters in front, the Wardens behind, and
the Past Masters on rising benches behind them.
Care was taken that the Lodges were ranked so
that the two Fraternities were completely intermixed. The two Fraternities had previously
assembled in two adjoining rooms, and having
opened two Grand Lodges, each according to its
peculiar solemnities, they passed to the Assembly
Hall in the following order :—

Grand Usher with his Staff.   Grand Usher with his Staff.
The Duke of Kent's Band of Music, fifteen in number,
all Masons, three and three.

Two Grand Stewards.   Two Grand Stewards.
A Cornucopia borne by a M.M. A Cornucopia borne by a M.M.
Two Grand Stewards.   Two Grand Stewards.
Two Golden Ewers by Master   Two Golden Ewers by Master
Masons.   Masons.
The nine worthy and expert   The nine worthy and expert
Masons, forming the Lodge of Masons, forming the Lodge of
Reconciliation, in single file, Reconciliation, in single file,
rank to rank, with the   rank to rank, with the
emblems of Masonry.   emblems of Masonry.
The Grand Secretary,   The Grand Secretary,
bearing the Book of Consti-   bearing the Book of Consti-
tutions and Great Seal.   tutions and Great Seal.

The Grand Treasurer with the Golden Key.
The Corinthian Light.
The pillar of the Junior Grand Warden on a pedestal.
The Junior Grand Warden with his gavel.
The Deputy Grand Chaplain, with the Holy Bible.
The Grand Chaplain.
Past Grand Wardens.

The Doric Light.
The pillar of the Senior Grand Warden on a pedestal.
The Senior Grand Warden with his gavel.
Two Past Grand Masters.
The Deputy Grand Master.
His Excellency the Count de Lagardje, the Swedish Ambassador, Grand Master of the first Lodge of the North, visitor.
The Royal Banner.
The Ionic Light.
The Grand Sword Bearer.
THE GRAND MASTER OF ENGLAND,
THE DUKE OF KENT, WITH THE ACT OF UNION IN DUPLICATE.
Two Grand Stewards.
Grand Tyler.

The Grand Treasurer with the Golden Key.
The Corinthian Light.
The pillar of the Junior Grand Warden on a pedestal.
The Junior Grand Warden with his gavel.

The Grand Chaplain with the Holy Bible.
Past Grand Wardens.
Provincial Grand Masters.
The Doric Light.
The pillar of the Senior Grand Warden on a pedestal.
The Senior Grand Warden with his gavel.

Acting Deputy Grand Master.

The Ionic Light.
The Grand Sword Bearer.
THE GRAND MASTER OF ENGLAND,
THE DUKE OF SUSSEX, WITH THE ACT OF UNION IN DUPLICATE.
Two Grand Stewards.
Grand Tyler.

Sir George Nayler, the Director of Ceremonies, having proclaimed silence, the Rev. Dr. Barry, Grand Chaplain to the fraternity under the Duke of Kent, offered solemn prayer, and Sir George read the Act of Union. Then the Rev. Dr.

Coghlan, after the sound of trumpet, proclaimed aloud : " Hear ye : This is the Act of Union, engrossed, in confirmation of articles solemnly concluded between the two Grand Lodges of Free and Accepted Masons of England, signed, sealed, and ratified by the two Grand Lodges respectively, by which they are to be hereafter and for ever known and acknowledged by the style and title of

THE UNITED GRAND LODGE OF ANCIENT FREE-
MASONS OF ENGLAND.

How say you, Brothers, representatives of the two Fraternities? Do you accept of, ratify, and confirm the same? " To which the assembly answered : " We do accept, ratify, and confirm the same." The Grand Chaplain then said : " And may the Great Architect of the Universe make the Union perpetual." To which all assembled replied : " So mote it be." Thereupon the two Grand Masters and the six Commissioners signed the deeds, and the Grand Masters affixed the great seals of their respective Grand Lodges to them. The trumpet again sounded, and the Rev. Dr. Barry, stepping forth, proclaimed : " Be it known to all men that the Act of Union between the two Grand Lodges of Free and Accepted Masons of England is solemnly signed, sealed, ratified, and confirmed, and the two Fraternities

are one, to be from henceforth known and acknowledged by the style and title of the United Grand
Lodge of Ancient Freemasons of England, and
may the Great Architect of the Universe make
their union perpetual." And the assembly said
" Amen." '

THE ARK OF THE COVENANT.

This was followed by a deeply impressive scene.
" The two Grand Masters, with their respective
Deputies and Wardens," says a contemporary
record, " advanced to the Ark of the Masonic
Covenant, prepared under the direction of Bro.
John Soane, R.A., Grand Superintendent of Works,
for the edifice of the union, and in all time to
come to be placed before the Throne. The Grand
Masters standing in the East, with their Deputies
on the right and left ; the Grand Wardens in
the West and South ; the Square, the Plumb,
the Level, and the Mallet were successively delivered to the Deputy Grand Masters, and by them
presented to the two Grand Masters, who severally,
applied the Square to that part of the Ark which
is square, the Plumb to the sides of the same,
and the Level above it in three positions ; and,
lastly, they gave three knocks with the Mallet,
saying, ' May the Great Architect of the Universe
enable us to uphold the Grand Edifice of Union,
of which the Ark of the Covenant is the symbol,

which shall contain within it the instrument of
our brotherly love, and bear upon it the Holy
Bible, Square and Compass, as the light of our
faith and the rule of our works. May He dispose
our hearts to make it perpetual.' And the Brethren
said : ' So mote it be.' The two Grand Masters
placed the said Act of Union in the interior of
the said ark. The cornucopia, the wine, and oil
were in like manner presented to the Grand
Masters, who, according to ancient rite, poured
forth corn, wine, and oil on this said ark, saying,
' As we pour forth corn, wine, and oil on this
Ark of the Masonic Covenant, may the bountiful
hand of Heaven ever supply this United Kingdom
with abundance of corn, wine, and oil, with all
the necessaries and comforts of life ; and may
He dispose our hearts to be grateful for all His
Gifts.' And the assembly said ' Amen.' "

THE LODGE OF RECONCILIATION.

It having been found impracticable, from the
shortness of notice, for the sister Grand Lodges
of Scotland and Ireland to send deputations to
the assembly according to the urgent request of
the two Fraternities, conferences had been held
with the most distinguished Grand Officers and
enlightened Masons resident in and near London,
in order to establish perfect agreement upon all

4

the essential points of Masonry, according to the ancient traditions and general practice of the Craft. The members of the Lodge of Reconciliation, accompanied by Count de Lagardje and Bro. Dr. Van Hess, and other distinguished Masons, withdrew to an adjoining room, where, being congregated and tyled, the result of all the previous conferences was made known.   Returning to the Temple, Count de Lagardje declared that the forms agreed on and settled by the Lodge of Reconciliation were pure and correct.   These forms were recognized as those " to be alone observed and practised in the United Grand Lodge and all the Lodges dependent thereon until Time shall be no more."   Then, the Holy Bible spread open, with the Square and Compasses thereon, was laid on the Ark of the Covenant, and the two Grand Chaplains approached.   The recognized obligation was then pronounced aloud by the Rev. Dr. Hemming, one of the Masters of the Lodge of Reconciliation, the whole of the Brethren repeating it after him, with joined hands, and declaring, " By this solemn obligation we vow to abide, and the regulations of Ancient Freemasonry now recognized strictly to observe."

THE FIRST UNITED GRAND LODGE.

The assembly next proceeded to constitute one Grand Lodge.   All the Grand Officers of the two

Fraternities having divested themselves of their
insignia, and Past Grand Officers having taken
the chairs, the Duke of Kent stated that when
he took upon himself the important office of Grand
Master of the Ancient Fraternity, his idea, as declared at the time, was to facilitate the important
object of the Union, which had that day been so
happily concluded.   And he now proposed that
his illustrious and dear relative, the Duke of
Sussex, should be the Grand Master of the United
Grand Lodge of Ancient Freemasons of England
for the year ensuing.   This having been seconded
by the Hon. Washington Shirley, and carried
unanimously and with Masonic honours, His Royal
Highness was placed on the Throne by the Duke
of Kent and Count de Lagardje, and solemnly
obligated.   The Grand Master then nominated his
officers : Rev. S. Hemming, D.D., S.G.W. ; Isaac
Lindo, J.G.W. ; John Dent, Grand Treasurer ;
William Meyrick, Grand Registrar ; William
Henry White and Edward Harper, Grand Secre-
taries ; Rev. Edward Barry, D.D., and Rev.
Lucius Coghlan, Grand Chaplains ; Rev. Isaac
Knapp, Deputy Grand Chaplain ; John Soane,
Grand Supt. of Works ; Sir G. Nayler, G.D.C. ;
Capt. Jonathan Parker, G. Sword Bearer ; Samuel
Wesley, G. Organist ; B. Aldhouse, G. Usher ;
and W. V. Salmon, G. Tyler.   It was then
solemnly proclaimed that the two Grand Lodges

were incorporated and consolidated into one, and
the Grand Master declared it to be open in due
form according to ancient usage. The Grand
Lodge was then called to refreshment, and from
the cup of brotherly love the Grand Master drank
to the Brethren, " Peace, Goodwill, and Brotherly
Love all over the World," and then passed the
cup. As it was going round, a choir sang a
piece of music specially composed for the occasion.

THE FIRST ACT OF GRAND LODGE.

The Grand Lodge was recalled to labour, and
as the first act of the United Fraternity, the Duke
of Sussex moved :—

That an humble address be presented to
H.R.H. the Prince Regent respectfully to
acquaint him with the happy event of the
reunion of the two great Grand Lodges of
the Ancient Freemasons of England, an event
which cannot fail to afford lively satisfac-
tion to their Illustrious Patron, who presided
for so many years over one of the Fraternities, and under whose auspices Freemasonry
has risen to its present flourishing condition.
That the unchangeable principles of the Insti-
tution are well known to His Royal Highness,
and the great benefits and end of this reunion are to promote the influence and opera-

tion of these principles by more extensively inculcating loyalty and affection of their Sovereign, obedience to the laws and magistrates of their country, and the practice of all the religious and moral duties of life, objects which must be ever dear to His Royal Highness in the government of His Majesty's United Kingdom. That they humbly hope and pray for the continuance of the sanction of His Royal Highness's fraternal patronage ; and that they beg leave to express their fervent gratitude for the many blessings which, in common with all their fellow-subjects, they derive from his benignant sway. That the Great Architect of the Universe may long secure these blessings to them and to their country by the preservation of His Royal Highness, their Illustrious Patron !

Resolutions thanking the Dukes of Kent and Sussex for " yielding to the prayer of the United Fraternities to take upon themselves the personal conduct of the negotiations for a reunion, which is this day, through their zeal, conciliation, and fraternal example so happily completed " ; and commending the proceedings of the day to Grand Lodges of Scotland and Ireland, were also passed before the Lodge was closed " in ample form and with solemn prayer."

II.—THE SOURCE OF SIGNS AND SYMBOLS.

By going back to primitive man, the Pygmy, we find the first symbol we use. He believed in the Supreme Spirit and propitiated elemental powers. In the stage of the Nilotic Negro we find more of our Signs and Symbols. Following the evolution to that of Totemic Sociology, and commencement of the Stellar Cult, we have still many more Signs, Symbols and Rites of our Order, and the whole tale of the Christian doctrines founded. Because it was amongst the Masai group in Inner Africa that the tradition arose, and *is still extant, that the Man-God came from Heaven, suffered, and was crucified and rose again.* We must remember that man at this time had very few words to express his ideas and beliefs ; it was done by signs and symbols, and Sign Language, and although this has been lost for thousands of years, it is now being rediscovered by men who can read this Sign Language. The Solar Cult and the Christian Cult, which have followed one another, have not in either case altered the tale, it is all one and the same from the beginning ; that names have altered is nothing, different languages have different names for the same idea, and because the attributes of the One Great God were expressed in "Zootype form" during the Stellar Cult, and "Gods and Goddesses" in the Solar, whilst at the present day

these are expressed in words, does not alter the
meaning, ideas, or beliefs ; these are only altered
and misunderstood by men who cannot read and
understand " The Writings on the Walls " ; and
as regards dates, few, I believe, now would even
think or believe that man has only existed about
six thousand years, as assumed from Biblical
tradition, when we find the skeletons of the present
type of man in strata of the Pliocene age, six
hundred thousand years old at least.[1]   Therefore
whatever Cult our Brothers may have belief in,
the knowledge of the evolution of the human race
would only be a greater factor to strengthen their
belief.   If we take the Chinese, and there are
many Brothers amongst them, we know that they
went out from Egypt during the Stellar Cult, and
they have never risen in evolution since.   The
Hindu left at the time of the Solar Cult ; he has
always remained the same.   The white race,
generally, left at the end of the Solar.   The early
Copts were the first of the Christians in evolution,
and the white man has gradually developed into a
higher type of the human.   With this development
into a higher type of man, so his spiritual ideas have
developed into a so-called higher type of Christianity than that which we find at the commencement of the time of the early Copts.   Yet it

[1] See "Genesis of Rocks and Ores," by Brenton Symons,
F.G.S., C.M.E.

is all one and the same from the beginning, under different names. The original Signs and Symbols which our early Brothers had to use in place of words, which they had not, have now given place to expressions in linguistic and grammatical form, of which they were, at that time, still ignorant. I am bound to bring this before my Brothers because I wish to assure them that I have no intention or wish to shake their faith in the Volume of the Sacred Law, but, quite on the contrary, wish to establish their faith still firmer, more especially those who profess the Christian doctrines, by proving that these are the highest point of the religious conception of the human in his progressive evolution.

That the dead were buried in the faith founded on the Mystery of the Cross over thirty thousand years ago is proved by the Pyramid of Medum and other remains still extant ; the so-called Tomb of Olham Fodhla, in Ireland, is an instance of this. The gnosis of the Crucifixion, however, was the same in the Stellar Cult three hundred thousand years before this, as is witnessed by the Pictograph taken from the Central American ruins (see Fig. 1). It is over two hundred thousand years old, and represents the Crucifixion during the period of the Stellar Cult. He is crucified on the two Poles—North and South. The Hieroglyphics state that He is the God of the North and South.

He is the Great One of the seven Glorious Ones (attributes). A Crown of Thorns is depicted on his head. His side is pierced with a spear, from whence blood and water is falling on his Spiritual Name, which, in Egyptian, is Amsu. He is sup-

The Crucified Victim.

FIG. I.

ported by his four brothers, Amsta, Hapi, Taumutf, and Kabhsenuf ; representing Matthew, Mark, Luke, and John of the Christians, represented by four squares. Tears are in his eyes, "Ye are the tears made by my eye in your name of men." I give the different names by which He was known in different countries, namely : Horus, of the Stellar Cult of the Egyptians ; Huitzilopochtli, of the Aztecs ; Zipe, of the Zapotics ; Hacaxipectli, of Guatemala ; Ptah-Seker-Ausar, of the Egyptians in their Solar Cult ; Tien-hwang Ta-Tici, of the Chinese ; Merodach, of the Babylonians ; Iu, or Ea, of the Chaldeans, Assyrians, and Druids of these Islands ; Uiracocha, of the Peruvians, and many other names in various parts of this world ; yet all one and the same, as proved by the same signs and symbols always associated with him in whatever part of the world found.

The signs and symbols herein portrayed read that He is the Great Lord and God of Heaven, situated at the North Pole ; He is God of the Pole Stars and God of the North and South, and the Heavens and Paradise, and his age is given as thirty-three years in the Mexican Codices 95 f. ; it is written in the Hieroglyphics of Egypt as thirty-three years.

The Eschatology of the Old Egyptians was " Their doctrines of Final Things," and they taught this to the Brothers by Signs and Symbols and various Rites and Ceremonies, in a dramatic form, the more to impress it upon the initiates. Their Code of Morals was the highest that has ever been promulgated by any nation. The Laws of Moses were the old laws of Egypt, which has been proved by finding the Stelae of Hammurabi, handed on from the Sumarians to the Babylonians. This Stelae was engraved at least two thousand years before Moses lived, and however much it may cause a shock to some people, it is true, because this Stelae is still extant. Our Brotherhood teaches the same, and in the same way. The proof can be seen in the Ritual of ancient Egypt.

Let us now see what the formations of these early Lodges were, and the reasons for the same ; the ceremony of their initiation ; and, lastly, their Signs, Symbols, Secret ,Words ; and the explanation and meaning of these. The Brothers throughout the world can then judge if my contention is not right.

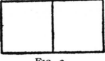

FIG. 2.

In the Old Stellar Cult, the primary formation was a circle. After, when the whole of the seven Lesser Mysteries were taught, the formation of the Temple was " a double square " end to end (Fig. 2), and the reason of this was because it represented Heaven as a square, and the Earth as a square, and the orientation of Temples was South for fifty-two thousand years ; then North for at least two hundred and fifty thousand years. In the centre of the Temple there were three cubes, one above the other (Fig. 3), representing the Primary Trinity. In some Temples these were ornamented by a double axe (Fig. 4). The Temples were sometimes called the House of the God of the Axe, in their language. The single axe, in Egyptian, is termed Neter, and may be translated as The Great One—Prince or Ruler is probably the correct translation. (The late Sir L. Page Renouf agreed with me in this translation.) Therefore we have these symbols representing The Great One of the North (i.e. Horus), The Great One of the South (i.e. Set), and The

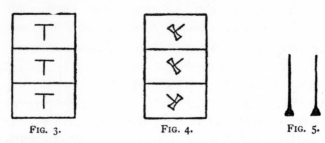

FIG. 3.   FIG. 4.   FIG. 5.

Great One of the Equinox (i.e. Shu), the Primary Trinity.

At the principal entrance of the Temples there were always Two Pillars. One was the Pillar of Set and the other was the Pillar of Horus, representing the two divisions of Heaven, North and South, and their portrayal was at first in the form of Fig. 5. On the top of the columns later (see Fig. 15) were four lines, which represented the Heaven as a square and the Earth as a square ; the Egyptians could not draw perspectively, but only on the flat, at this early period. At the present day these are represented by the Celestial and Terrestrial Globes.

Now this was the form of every Temple throughout the world, and at the porchway entrance these two Columns always stood ; in whatever country these ruins are found the form is the same ; it is also the correct form of a Masonic Lodge, and, as is well known, these two Columns stood at the porchway entrance of King Solomon's Temple and bore the names of J. and B.

These two Pillars, in Egypt, were placed at the porchway of all Temples in the Solar Cult to represent the entrance of their Amenta ; one was called Tatt, the other Tattu. The word Tattu also denotes the two Tatt Pillars. The Tatt is a figure of stability ; it supports the four corners, and is equal to the Square. Thus two Tatts at the entrance to Tattu is equivalent to a Double Square. Tattu is the entrance or gateway to the region where the mortal Soul is blended with the Immortal Spirit, and thereby established for ever.

According to the Egyptian wisdom all these Temples were simply representatives, so to speak, of their Heaven. Their Priests were human representatives of the Divine Master in his various attributes, and bore Divine titles—the same as the Principal O's in some of our degrees. Their teachings, forms, and ceremonies represented their

beliefs as to the life that must be led on this
earth to attain the everlasting life of happiness
in the next ; and the trials the Spirit would be
subjected to until that end was accomplished.

Although the form of our Lodges and the Ancient
Temples is the same, also the two Pillars or
Columns at the entrance, we do not have in our
M.M. Lodges the Cubes in the Centre ; but the
R.A. does, the reason being that we have divided
the " seven Ancient Mysteries " in a different
manner than did our ancient Brethren.

FIG. 6.   FIG. 7.   FIG. 8.

The Triangle was sacred on account of its
representing Heaven. The Primary Triangle was
as No. 1, Fig. 6 ; and originally represented Set,
the God of the South (El Shaddai of the Phœnicians), and was, in fact, an Ideograph for his
name. Horus, the God of the North, was also
represented by a triangle, as No. 2, Fig. 6, which
is also an Ideograph for his name. Later, when
Horus became Primary God, the Egyptians associated all the attributes of Set to him, including
the Triangle of Set, and this was then depicted as
in Fig. 7, which is a later type of Fig. 8.

Amongst the oldest Brotherhood the two double triangles (Fig. 8) were surrounded by four Uraei as guardians of the same ; at a later phase it was three double triangles, surrounded with concentric circles. At the entrance of their Temples there were always " two watchers," each armed with a knife. The one outside the door was called the Watcher ; the one inside the door was called the Herald, as seen in the Veginetta.

The Egyptian initiatory ceremony was conducted with great secrecy and care. The candidates were divested of most of their clothing, and a chain, or rope of some kind, placed around their neck, to signify their belief in God, their dependence on Him, and their solemn obligations to submit and devote themselves to His will and service. The fact that they were neither naked nor clothed was an emblem that they were untutored men, children of nature, unregenerate, and destitute of any knowledge of the true God, as well as being destitute of the comforts of life. The chain or rope was a symbol that the candidate was being led from darkness to light, from ignorance to a knowledge of the One True and Living God, Creator, and Judge of all things in Heaven and Earth. The candidate was blindfolded, and then led by a brother (called in Egyptian An-er-f) to the door of the Temple or Lodge, which appeared as a blank wall in the form of A, Fig. 9. Arriving at this door he asked for admittance, and was asked by the "watcher" who he was. His answer, translated from the Egyptian, was "The Kneeler," i.e. Shu. He was then given a password which, in Egyptian, is Ra-gririt. The door was an

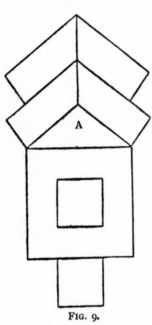

equilateral triangle, a symbol typical of Heaven. The square on which he trod as he passed through was a symbol typical of Earth ; the whole entrance symbolized passing from Earth to Heaven. The candidate was then conducted through long passages, and round the Lodge seven times ; he had to answer various questions, words of " power and might " being given him. Finally, he was conducted to the centre of the Lodge and asked what he desired mostly ; his answer was that Light might be given him. The candidate had to commence his perambulations with his left foot first, the reason for which is given in the Papyrus of Nesi-Amsu, which gives the destruction of Apap,

FIG. 9.

PLATE A.

Grand Master's Apron and Collar. Satit presents the Pharaoh Amenothes III to Khnûmû. (Drawn by Faucher-Gudin from one of the bas-reliefs of the Temple of Khnûmû, at Elephantine. This is now destroyed.)

To face p. 49.

the greatest serpent of Evil. The left foot was first placed on him, and is symbolical of commencing our journey through life by putting all evil thoughts and actions under and away from us ; we should tread down the great evils which beset us through life. The destruction of Apap is given in these words which can be found in the Papyrus of Nesi-Amsu : " His body shall be cut in pieces and burnt to ashes, and these ashes scattered over the face of the earth and water by the four winds of Heaven."

If the candidate turned back, or violated his obligations, his Throat was cut and Head chopped off (Ritual, Ch. xc.) after his Heart had been torn out (Ritual, Ch. xxvii., xxviii., and xl.). These Mysteries were the beliefs of the old wise men of Egypt enacted in a dramatic form to teach the Initiates their beliefs, as to what the Soul, or Manes, had to undergo or pass through after he had departed this Earthly life, before he could enter Paradise.

Their W..M., or High Priest, was placed in his chair with the same Grip and Token as we use at the present day, except that it was the other Arm, as may be seen on one of the bas-reliefs of the Temple of Khnûmû, at Elephantine. Here the W.M.E. is presented to the master in the chair, who then places him in his chair with the Grip and Token, and gives him the word of the Chair,

5

which in Egyptian is Maat-Heru, meaning " One whose voice must be obeyed."

The emblem of Power and Might which is given to the W.M.—the Gavel—took its origin from the original sacred sign still used amongst the Pygmies in Inner Africa (Fig. 10). It is their symbol for The Great One, The Chief. It is just three sticks crossed.

The Nilotic Negroes, who followed the Pygmy all over the world, converted the crossed sticks

FIG. 10.   FIG. 11.   FIG. 12.

into a double cross (Fig. 11) by placing the two sticks in a different way.

In a later phase it was used as a symbol to represent the Great One, the Great Prince, in the form of a double-headed Hammer or Axe (Fig. 12), when stones took the place of these crossed sticks, and primitive man began to acquire the knowledge of hafting [(Nilotic Negroes).

In the Third, or M.M. degree, the death of H.A.B., and the legend attached thereto, is not borne out by facts, as we see from 2 Chron. iv. 11 :

PLATE B.

*Master's Apron and Collar.   The Pharaoh
Menkauhou.   (Drawn by Boudier from
a photograph by Faucher-Gudin.)*

To face p. 50.

PLATE C.

Companions (F.C.) Apron. Stele in the form of a door and the Statue of the Tomb of Minuka. (Drawn by Boudier from a photograph by M. de Morgan.)

" And Hiram finished the work that he was to make for King Solomon for the House of God " ; and Josephus mentions that " he lived at Tyre long afterwards." It is an innovation made by those who could not understand the Egyptian prototype, when it originated.

The old Brothers of Egypt wore leather aprons, as do Freemasons of to-day, only of a different shape. The Egyptian apron was triangular, the strings or sash being fixed at the apex. They also wore collars. One apron, which I have seen, was that of the High Priest. It was yellowish-white in colour, made of leather, with tassels of gold, bearing the name of Amsu with an emerald stone in the centre. The collars worn by the High Priests were of gold, while another suspended collar bore twelve different stones, set in gold, representing the twelve divisions of Heaven, or the Signs of the Zodiac. As there were various degrees—seven in the Lesser Mysteries and ten in the Greater Mysteries—so the aprons and ollars varied in colour and ornamentation as they do with modern Masonry.

The G.W. in our thirtieth degree, as now given, and which we are informed is to be found in Maccabees (but that is not so), is, in Egyptian, " Montu-anhûri," the meaning of both the ancient and modern word being identical.

The origin of the term " Companions " dates

at least six hundred thousand years or more. It was first used in the time of the Totemic Sociology, before the Stellar Cult was evolved, which we may term Monumental times. Egypt was first divided into Nomes or Domains ; one of these Nomes was called *Ariu*—the land of the Ari. It was the seventeenth Nome of Upper Egypt, and the only one which supplied workmen for the Temples. These Ari were styled "Companions," because they worked in Companies, and were initiated in the first and second degrees, and *these were the originals of the " Operative Masons."* None of them were initiated beyond the third mystery, and they were quite a distinct class from the " Old Religious Brotherhood," who employed them to build their Temples and initiated them so that they should keep the secrets of the same. A body of these left Egypt at the time of the Stellar Cult and travelled throughout the world wherever the Stellar Priests went ; the first exodus was by the Botyia, the next by the Turanians. A Priest who was initiated into the third always accompanied them, though he was not an Operative himself.

The buildings of these old Stellar people can always be identified in whatever part of the world found. These were always iconographic, which the people who followed did not copy. Both the Stellar and Solar built in polygonal and monolithic forms, stones, but the Solar was never iconographic.

One of the earliest Ideographs for Set, El Shaddai, and Horus were the two Eyes [(see Fig. 13), symbols of the two Pole Stars, North and South, originating at Apta, or at the Mount of the Equinox—Equatorial Africa. Another Ideograph was the two Poles—the Pole or Pillar of the South, assigned to Set, and the Pillar or Pole of the North, assigned to Horus (Fig. 15), the two Tatt Pillars. The Ideograph for the name of Set, as El Shaddai, was as No. 1, Fig. 6, and that for the name of Horus was as No. 2,

FIG. 13.   FIG. 14.   FIG. 15.

Fig. 6. Fig. 10 was also an Ideographic Symbol for Horus, as Amsu, but was never attached to, or associated with, the God Set or El Shaddai.

The reason why the Operative Masons have gone wrong in this part of their ritual is that they have mixed up the Gods of the four quarters with the One Great God. These only represented attributes ; and they have also mixed up the God of the Pole Star South, El Shaddai, with the God of the Pole Star North, which was Horus, or Ihuh, of Israel, or Iu, Ea, of the Chaldeans, Assyrians, and Babylonians, which is later than the Sumarian

El Shaddai of the Egyptian Set. These four Gods of the four quarters were, first, the brothers, and, secondly, the children of Horus ; in Egyptian, Amsta, Hapi, Taumutf, and Kabhsnuf ; in Mexican, Acatl, Tecpatl, Calli, and Tochtli ; the four Bacabs of the Mayas ; the Man, Lion, Ox, and Eagle of the R.A.C., and Matthew, Mark, Luke, and John of the Christians.

That the Operative Masons have seven so-called degrees now is because they have converted their Initiate, Apprentice, and Master's degrees into seven ; but this is of quite a comparatively recent date. The Initiates and Apprentices were called "Companions," and a few of the higher class were "Masters." Bro. Dr. Carr has stated that the reasons for much of the Speculative Ceremonies can be seen in the Operative Rituals, while the Operative Ceremonies get no elucidation from the Speculative Ritual, and he specially draws attention to the obligation in the First Degree. The reason for this is obvious. *The Operative Masons or "Companions" were initiated in part of the old Ceremonies and Rituals* only, so that they were bound by Oath to keep the secrets of, and know the reasons for, the peculiar and distinctive construction of the old Temples, and they never violated their obligations ; but the Operative Masons have no Esoteric Eschatological rites at all. These were never taught them, *yet these*

existed before the Operatives—when the old
Temples were formed by a simple double circle
of stones, twelve in number for each, surrounded
by bushes. Thus a Brother who understands and
knows all the ten Greater Mysteries, knows and
understands all the Operative Masons' work, whilst
the latter are completely ignorant as to the former.

But the Operative Masons' origin dates back
at least six hundred thousand years, and so I have
no doubt they will be contented with their great
antiquity. The proofs of all my contentions are in
the Ritual of Ancient Egypt, and on the various
monuments ; these I shall always be pleased to
identify and point out to any Brother who may
feel interested in this subject. The Operative
Masons, like the Speculative, have made many
" innovations " since they left Old Mother Egypt,
but this is not surprising considering all the vicis-
situdes they have passed through ; the wonder is
that so much remains of the original, and that so
little innovation has taken place after all these
years, remembering the trials and tribulations
they have endured.

Our 24-inch gauge is the old cubit of the ancient
Egyptians. It is the ideographic hieroglyphic, and
has the phonetic value of Maat, and indicated,
primarily, " that which is straight," and was the
name given to the instrument by which the work
of the " Craftsmen " was kept straight and

measured ; metaphorically, a rule, or law, or canon, by which the lives of men and their actions were kept straight and governed. The ancient Brothers thus used the word in a physical and moral sense, as their naming it Maat clearly proves, therefore it is an important instrument, analogous to our own, much more so than the majority of the Brothers would conceive.

The British inch was the unit of linear measurement used at the building of the Great Pyramid, or at least it is the nearest standard in existence, as it has lost one one-thousandth part of itself after being carried from land to land all these thousands of years. There is, therefore, more in it than being an instrument to " measure our work " and being " symbolical of time." One inch is the time representation of the Great Year prophetically. Five hundred millions of the Pyramid inch is the length of the earth's Polar diameter. Twenty-five inches give the length of the Sacred Cubit, $5 \times 5 = 25$ angles of the Pyramid. The absolute length of the Sacred Cubit is the same used by the Israelites and spoken of in the V.S.L. as the one ordained by God, and was brought out of Egypt by Moses, who, being one of the High Priests of On, knew and understood the Mysteries and Secrets of the Great Pyramid and the Sacred Doctrines. It was different in length to that of the Greek, Roman, and latter-day Egyptian Cubit.

Freemasons, perhaps, unknown to most of themselves, have been the custodians of the secrets connected with it from the original, through ages of time. Thus we see that the standard and unit of linear measurement, used at the building of the Great Pyramid (during the Stellar Cult), from which the British inch was derived in primeval days of purity and Eschatological worship, before the people fell away from their true doctrines, has been handed down by us pure and unsullied. The Incas, Mayas, and all the Old Stellar Cult people before them, possessed and used this same measure. The great attempt of the French people to abolish alike the Christian religion and hereditary weights and measures of all nations ; to replace the former by worship of philosophy, and the latter by the metre (the French metre scheme depending, in a certain manner of their own, upon the magnitude of the earth), is not very old, nor yet an improvement upon the exactness in measurement of these Egyptian people ; because, by assuming as their unit and standard of length, the one ten-millionth of a "quadrant of the earth's surface," that took a curved line drawn on the earth's surface, in place of the straïght axis of rotation, it could not be so exact, and, in fact, is far inferior in measurement. The British hereditary inch, therefore, is much nearer and more exact to an integral earth measure. As long as one retains a power of geometry, so

long will the diameter be thought of greater
primary importance than the circumference of a
circle ; and when we come to a sphere in motion,
the axis of its dynamical labour shall hold a vastly
superior importance, especially when the earth's
equator is not a true circle. Thus we see that
this symbol has a great claim upon our attention,
and we have to return to the Egyptians of the
Stellar Cult for its origin.

The origin of the Blazing Star was the Egyptian
"Sothos," and is shown in Zootype form as
Anubis, who guided the souls through the Under-
world, and its allusion as the Star which guided
the Wise Men is a recent version of the old (see
Ritual). In another form, as "The Bright Morning
Star"—the Star with eight rays—it represents
Horus of the resurrection. It was typified by
Orion, the eightfold one, the highest of the seven,
with the essence of these to make One—The One,
therefore eight. In Revelation the Son of God
promises to give the Morning Star to him that
overcometh ; "as I also have received of my
Father ; and I will give Him the Morning Star"
(Rev. ii. 28). The Morning Star was equally
identified with Horus ; "I know the power of the
East ; Horus of the Solar Mount ; the Calf in
the presence of God ; and the Star of Dawn"
(Ritual, Ch. cix.). Henceforth the Morning Star

was given to the followers of Horus, therefore, we, as descendants of the original brothers and followers of Horus, still retain the symbol.

It was the Star of Horus, and his guide, which led him to Paradise when he seated himself upon his Throne, and then Horus gave his Star as a guide to his followers (see Ritual). In one representation in the Egyptian he is seen with the Star on his head, beckoning on his followers.

The Masonic Square is depicted in many of the Ancient Temples, and also in the Great Pyramid. In the Egyptian Hall of Judgment Osiris is seated on the Square whilst judging the dead. It is also portrayed as the corner-stone of the building, and as the Foundation of Eternal Law in the Court of Divine Justice. The Egyptian name of it is Neka. It was first employed in squaring the stones of the builders, and symbolically in squaring the conduct in the sphere of morals of the Brotherhood. Maat is also depicted as sitting on the Square. Thus we have this symbol bearing the same interpretation as in Masonry. Among the Egyptians, when it was employed in squaring the stones of the builder, it denoted Creation according to Eternal Laws or understanding rules, it was the seat of Justice, and of judging right from wrong, " To bring the material into perfect form and to reject that which was not perfect, both physically and morally." To build on the Square as a fourfold foundation, is to build for ever. Some of the Operative Masons were classed and called, in Egyptian, Stone-squarers.

The ancients used the rough and smooth Ashlar as much as we do. The smooth Ashlar, or Cube, symbolically represented and signified Truth. The twelve Camps and the twelve Banners of the Children of Israel represent the original characters in their Astronomical Mythology, and were given first to the twelve Thrones or divisions of Heaven in the Stellar Cult, and in the Zodiac, in the final. Thus at first they represented twelve Stellar powers, and around many Temples we find these twelve depicted by Pillars of Stone. The original characters in the Astronomical Mythology, that were given the twelve Thrones or Camps, with separate and distinctive Banners, or Totemic Zoo-types, were : Sut, Horus, Shu, Hapi, Ap-Uat, Kabhsenuf, Amsta, Anup, Ptah, Atum, Sau, Hu. These were the Kamite originals, brought over and converted into the Banners of the twelve Camps or Tribes of Israel.

The four principal Banners in the R.A.C. took their origin from the four Brothers, or Children of Horus. They are to be found all over the world, wherever the Stellar Cult existed, and appear under a great variety of names.

The origin of the F.C. Sign has been given on page 340, " Signs and Symbols of Primordial

Man," and the origin of the D.C. Symbol on page 307.

None of our passwords are of pure Egyptian language, because these were lost for thousands of years ; we use many Hebrew words which mean the same as the Egyptian. I have discovered the old secret words, some of which I have given you. The true word for the Master's chair is Maat Heru—" One whose voice must be obeyed."

The first worker in Metals was not T.C.; the P.W. in Egyptian is Horus-Behutet, but any Brother who is interested will find all in the Ritual of Ancient Egypt. Dr. E. A. Wallis Budge, in " The Gods of the Egyptians," page 485, states : " It is, of course, impossible to say who were the ' blacksmiths ' that swept over Egypt from South to North, or where they came from," but believes " that they represent the invaders in predynastic times, who made their way into Egypt from a country in the East, by way of the Red Sea, and by some road across the eastern desert—that is, through the Wâdi Hammâmât. They brought with them the knowledge of working in metals and of brick-making, and having conquered the indigenous people in the South—i.e., those round about Edfu—they made that city the centre of their civilization, and then proceeded to conquer and occupy other sites and to establish sanctuaries for their God."

But I have proved that man originated in Africa and not Asia ("Origin and Evolution of Primitive Man "), and these came up from the South—Nilotic Negroes, the Kaverondo tribes. Remnants of these still exist in Africa. These were workers in iron and copper ; and amongst these people the blacksmiths are called "Yothetth " ; there is also a separate class called "Uvino," and amongst the Gemi Tribe the blacksmiths were founded into a religious secret society, and still possess all the secrets of Horus of Edfu.   Horus was their Great Chief in their Hero-Cult, and is the Chief Artificer in Metals —i.e. he was recognized as "the Chief Hero " of this Clan or Secret Society, in the time of the Totemic Sociology.

It must be interesting to know that amongst the Nilotic Negroes, and natives of South Africa, when they wish to convey the fact that they are speaking the absolute truth, or when they have as now sometimes to swear in a court of law that they are speaking the truth, they draw the right hand with fingers extended (some the index finger alone) across the throat, accompanied by the words, "Nisho i nkiso e perzulu," or if they omit the words, as amongst some tribes, they point upwards with the index finger and thumb extended, the other fingers being flexed upon the palm.   The words mean, "God cut my throat if I break this oath or do not tell the truth." It is the most binding oath of natives in Africa.

Many of our signs and secrets exist amongst these African people at the present day, and have been handed down from generation to generation by the old Turanians. It was these "blacksmith men" who knew how to smelt iron ore and forge the metal into weapons of offence and defence, that formed themselves into the "big clan of blacksmiths," having Horus as their Astronomical Chief. They came up from the South to the North in predynastic times, and, having conquered the Masaba Negroes and lower types of Nilotic Negroes, who were then the inhabitants of the land of Egypt, established themselves in Egypt, making Edfu their chief city and centre.

The Egyptians called these "followers of Horus" Mesnitu, or Mesniti, which, I believe, was the original name for all their tribes, and which may now be applied to the Masai Group. As we know, Horus was their deified God, and as Edfu became their centre, he was styled "Lord of the Forge City," "The Great Master Blacksmith." It was here that they first built a sanctuary or temple, which was called Mesnet. One hieroglyphic which they used (Fig. 16) proves that these people were those belonging to the Masai ancestors. Priests were appointed to attend to the Temple. One might say

FIG. 16.

that this was the first representative of our
Masonic Temple. Those who erected and looked
after the construction of the Temple were
styled " Companions." Thus we see that our word
T.C. is a substituted name. The original and
real " Great Master in Metals " was " Horus of
Edfu "—or ⸺" Horus-Behutet." I have given the
above fully as an example of the falsity of some
of the secret names we have substituted for the
originals. Many other words which we have
adopted have no relation or meaning to the
originals.

But the meaning of the mysteries could only be
known whilst the genuine gnosis was authentically
taught. This had ceased when the Christian
Sarcolatry literalized the mystic drama of Amenta,
the Earth of Eternity, as a more tangible-looking
human history and a new revelation sent from
God. Yet it is at least six hundred thousand
years old. From these mysteries the ceremonies
of the Masonic Brotherhood have been handed
down from generation to generation ; re-edited
and altered only to conform with our present ideas
—as, for instance, the statement : " The six periods
of the world's existence, now about to close with
the second advent, when time shall be swallowed
up in Eternity," has no meaning, nor has it any
significance in its present form.

The Great Pyramid of Egypt and Stellar Cult

explain the Mystery. The key to its meaning is the Seven Pole Stars, and the periods of precession of the same, which was also figured as Seven Eyes or Seven Circles, in consequence of these being a figure of a Cycle.

As a mode of measuring time and periods of the Great Year by the Stellar Cult, the eye or circle came to the full " as at first " seven times at seven stations of the Pole, in the Cycle of Precession. As a type the Eye might be full, once a month, once a quarter, once a year, once in a thousand years ; in 2,155 years ; 3,716 years, or in the Great Eye of All—The Eye of the Eternal once in 25,827 years (Ritual, Ch. cxl.-cxiv.).

The submergence of seven Pole Stars involved the same number of deluges, and marked the periods of the world's existence in the Cycle of Precession, which culminated in the great deluge of all, *not to be swallowed up in Eternity, but to recommence again* (only to be swallowed up in Eternity when the Pole Stars cease to exist). The Mystery of the seven Circles is the same as the Mystery of the seven Stars of Revelation ; it is the Mystery of the Celestial Heptanomes in the Stellar Cult of the old Egyptians.

The " Second Advent " marks the time of origin of this, which was at the time that these old teachers had marked the end of the second revolution of the seven Pole Stars (Ursa Minor), from the time of their first observing and recording. The proof of which they have left in Egypt on the monuments and in the Ritual—observations lasting up to that time 51,654 years, or two revolutions. Therefore, " the six periods of the world's existence were represented by the six Pole Stars in Precession, with the seventh added, which, when ended, or about to change to re-precession, represented the Great Deluge or Eternity of the Great Year, when all was at an end, to recommence again with another life or precession." It was astronomical mythology at first, a deluge being the ending of a cycle of time. It became a natural type of an ending of time in the uranographic representation, but in no other than in an astronomical sense of re-beginning at the same point of departure as in the beginning. It will re-begin again in the great circle of precession, but only as a matter of chronology.

In the great year of precession there were seven stations of the celestial pole, in these constellations : 1, Draconis ; 2, the Lesser Bear ; 3, Kepheus ; 4, Cygnus ; 5, Lyra ; 6, Hippopotamus ; and 7, Herakles (the Man). These were the seven sustaining powers of Heaven, the seven Pillars, seven Mounts, seven divinities, called Lords of Eternity. The circuit of precession first outlined by the movement of the celestial pole was the circle of the

eternal—or seven eternals—which they imaged by,
the Shennu-ring.   The end of the Great Year,
determined by the deluge of all, occurred in the
sign or constellation of the Man.   Hence when
they, converted their Stellar into Solar Cult, the
Brothers of the 18°, not knowing the true gnosis,
have fallen into a grave and nonsensical error,
which they still practise and carry on.

The seventeenth and eighteenth chapters of the
Ritual must be interesting to the Brethren of the
18°, because here we find in one of the ceremonies
of the old brotherhood the candidate had the veil
of darkness (a net) over his head, so that he was
unable to see. With the assistance of (in Egyptian)
Se-meri-f, he was led or had to pass through difficulties, danger, and darkness, after which he was
presented to the Great Circle of Princes or Chiefs,
the veil being removed by Thoth, who restored him
to light, life, health, and strength, and all the
glorious company of Princes, in which he was given
a place. He was first presented and conducted by
An-maut-ef, who saith : " I am come to you, ye
great circle of Princes in Heaven, upon earth, and
in the world below ; I bring to you N—, void of
offence towards any. Grant that he may be with
you daily." He is conducted by Se-meri-f through
the valley of the shadow of death, and after mount-
ing seven steps is presented to the Glorious Princes
with these words : " I come to you a circle of

Princes, and I bring N— to you'; Grant to him
bread, water, and air (provender of the altars) and
an allotment (or seat) in the Sechit-hotep, like
Horus." Thoth having removed the dark net, he
is invited to unite, or join in, the circle, and feast.
He states : " I have given bread to the hungry,
water to the thirsty, clothes to the naked, and a
boat to the shipwrecked." " Most Illustrious "
is an Egyptian title used for the Master of Masters
(Ritual, Ch. xiv.).

We have likewise mixed up our degrees into
thirty-three, some part of the first original seven
are now intermixed with so-called Higher Degrees.
The original Degrees were seven Lesser and ten
Greater. The seven Lesser belonged to and originated with the Old Stellar Cult. The ten Greater
belonged to and took their origin in the Solar Cult.
Some of our Signs and Symbols date back to
Primary Man, and in tracing his evolution we
find how these have originated and one added to
others, and how some of these have been changed
with the different Cults.

If we merely consider the tokens of recognition,
the passwords, secret words, and the decorations
of the Lodges, according to the degrees into which
modern Masonry is divided, we find that many
of them are taken from the V.S.L'., and are symbolical of events, real or imaginary, some of which
are said to have taken place in those comparatively

modern times which followed the decline and
destruction of the old Egyptian Empire, and
marked the commencement of the Christian era ;
others as having occurred before the Christian
Cult commenced, others at the building of King
Solomon's Temple, all of which some think, and
have stated, have nothing to do with the
Religious Mysteries of the Egyptians that were
in existence ages before. Where do those who
positively affirm that all these have not been derived from the Egyptians suppose they originated?
From whence did the above obtain them? It is
open to all students to confirm these observations
and translations, or to bring forward further
evidence in which they will critically demonstrate
that the photographs I have taken of these Signs
and Symbols still existing on the walls of Ancient
Temples and walls of ruined cities, in Africa, Asia,
Central, North, and South America, as well as
other parts of the world, have nothing whatever
to do with those in use amongst ourselves. Yet
these are identical in every form and shape, whatever may have been the esoteric meaning given
to them by the initiated of these countries.
Further, the translations of these old Rituals, which
we have now discovered and can read, are
analogous to our own ; at the same time, many
innovations have naturally been made because it
became necessary to replace those that were lost,

and to meet a higher state of evolution which man has now attained.

The proofs I have here brought forward are sufficient to prove my contention critically ; yet there are still many more to be found in " Signs and Symbols of Primordial Man " and the Ritual of Ancient Egypt, and I now leave it to all my Brother Masons to say, after a critical examination of the evidences, if my contention is justified or not.

II

THE SOUL OF MASONRY

CAN the unity of the world be accomplished by Freemasons? Yes ; and by Freemasons only. But not yet. That is the answer. Why not yet? is the question to be answered. One of the reasons is because the majority of Freemasons do not in reality carry out in daily practice the sublime tenets of the Brotherhood. And why? There are many reasons. I will try and enumerate some for the good of my brother Freemasons, and I hope that this may bear fruit both here and in foreign lands.

FIRST.—Because the *historical* aspect of Freemasonry is not known except to a few students of the Craft. The majority of the Brotherhood have been, and are, content to think that the history of Freemasonry is entirely modern. They have never studied it ; have never thought what it was, and is. We have no history of the Craft for those who cannot read ancient writings, except where I have given them a decipherment and translation of these, which probably many have never heard of, and few have read.

Beyond my works there is no history of Freemasonry, save in its modern aspects, except that which is disclosed in ancient writings. Few Brothers have studied the history of the human race and evolution of man, which alone contains the secret of the development of Freemasonry. If Freemasons studied this, even only in a minor degree, they would see and understand the evolution, or rather revolution, that is now taking place in this country at the present time, and which, if continued in its present phase for a few more years, will throw them back again, in the British Isles at least, to that chaos from which Freemasonry has many times already suffered. Without a knowledge of the past there cannot be any guide to the future. The present and continuous thought of our Brotherhood, as well as of others amongst the majority, is one of self, and great indifference to the feelings and welfare of others, except when it specially affects themselves, and it is here we have the

SECOND CAUSE.—Those of the Craft who are striving to bring about that high ideal of brotherhood to be a reality, and not a sham, are not supported with that fraternal activity which is so desirable. There are many Brothers who care nothing but to gain honours, which are a sham

to many who wear them.   Others only think of
Charity.   So far, that is right and good, but that
is not Freemasonry; nor will ever Freemasonry
be advanced further in the evolution or the
coalescing of the Brotherhood into one great
fraternal and universal whole by it.

The men of the various Governments all the
world over *think nothing of the true benefit of
the human race* ; with them it is party, politics, a
repetition of self, position, and aggrandisement,
to be obtained at any cost.   Possibly, if they
have ever studied the rise and fall of nations,
they may be conceited enough to try and abase
their thoughts and obliterate their better-thinking
powers, and so, deceiving themselves, make themselves believe that they cannot, or will not, fall
into the same evils which have followed every
nation that has entered on a similar course.   Vain,
ignorant, and foolish thoughts and actions, opposed
to the divine laws of nature, can only have one
result and termination.

In the past history of the world there are *two
causes* only, or primary factors, which paved the
way for the downfall and destruction of every
empire.

The first is the dissension of the Priests amongst
themselves, and, as a result which must naturally
follow such dissensions, the introduction of
Socialism.   *No people have ever risen to be a*

great nation and then fallen and been destroyed, except for these two causes. This is now being enacted again in this Empire, the greatest the world has ever seen. Are there any persons—any Brothers in our great fraternity—so foolish as to think that we can escape that doom and destruction which are awaiting us by continuing on such a course? The result and effect on Freemasonry cannot be expressed and demonstrated adequately in this work. Every Freemason who has had any experience knows the bitterness and vindictiveness with which the Roman Catholic Church treats the Brotherhood—and how much greater, if possible, will be the effect of the introduction of Socialism, which is fast pervading and threatening to eat the life out of our country. This is one phase of imminent and actual danger that is threatening our Brotherhood in a very acute form ; it is actual, it is real, however much we may wish to close our eyes, or however much indifference we may assume.

Only a few years ago we, in this country, went through great and acute tension—that danger which threatened war between us and the United States of America. That has passed, and will never return in an acute form again. Why? Because the Brotherhood sent their great representative, the Grand Master of Illinois, to this country, and I had the great pleasure to meet him at the Q. C.

L'odge, when he gave the message of peace and
brotherhood : "There shall be no war between
the United States of America and England ; we
are of one Brotherhood, and the Freemasons of
U.S.A. have decided that there shall be no war,
now or ever, between the two countries, and I am
delegated to come here and tell you this, representing over a million of Brothers, and ask you
in return to say there shall be no war." What
a glorious triumph for the Brotherhood !

Did the authorities who at present govern us
try and bring about the same result with the
recent friendly deputation of the Brotherhood
from Germany, or only talk platitudes—or were
they unsuccessful in their endeavours? [1]

We boast of a grand and perfect organization of
our great Brotherhood. Have we any organization that we can rely upon? Have we any leaders
of men? How many in those who govern the
Craft? How many Brothers have we who work,
and wish, and act for the one universal Brotherhood?

If our great Brotherhood were the perfect
organization that many suppose, with a government of " leaders of men " whose ambition was
only for the good of the Craft, the peace of the
world, with the universal fraternal relations which

---

[1] We know now that they were, for since writing the above
War has been declared ; it is unnecessary to dilate on it.

our tenets profess, there would be no war; there would be no downfall. We are numerous enough, we are strong enough, to govern the world, but we are not universally organized, and without this we are useless and impotent to form that unity of universal brotherhood which characterized Freemasonry two hundred thousand years ago. The mere talking of platitudes, what we are, and what we ought and wish to be, is useless without action, and yet there is apparently no action at present. We have numbers of great and good men in our ranks, and many in the Grand Councils and Governing bodies. Let them take action; the whole of the Brotherhood will support them. No Generals will ever have had such a devoted and large army as our Brotherhood will prove themselves to be. Let them lead with resolute action, and fear nothing, true to the principles of the Craft, without fear or favour, pure and unsullied; without sword, blow, or shedding of a tear, that great ideal would be accomplished. There can be no fear of the dissentient Priesthood now.

We have no dogmas or creeds to confuse the faith and belief in the One Great Eternal and Divine Architect of the Universe, Creator of All Things, therefore no question of a difference of creed would obtrude itself, or cause any secession amongst the Brothers of various climes and countries.

As for Politics—What antics do some creatures, calling themselves men, descend to for party reasons ! The grandest of all the Divine Creator's works—Man—has been degenerated into the basest of animals. Many, a disgrace to humanity, have no thoughts of the hereafter, or no real wish for the advancement of their fellow-creatures. What they profess is one thing, but what their actions denote is something totally antithetic.

I say, therefore, to all Freemasons throughout the world, organize under leaders of men who will act without fear or favour ; each one of you be true to the grand Brotherhood ; be true to the tenets of the Craft, and let these be a guide to your daily life, ever remembering that we are all of one Brotherhood, which is beyond any words to express. Life here is short, the life to come is for eternity. Try and think what eternity is. By your universal combination you possess the dominant power for the advancement and good of humanity generally. If you exercise these powers, the Divine Creator will be with you, will prosper and assist you. If you fail in this and " bury your talents," He will disperse and scatter you, as He has done before, and wait until other and more enlightened generations of the human family arise and take your place.

III

OUT OF THE SILENCE

Two very interesting articles on the Great Pyramid by Mr. F. E. Leith, of New Zealand, appeared in *The Freemason*—some of many that have been written on this subject—but his are of great importance and interest. It is a pity, however, that Mr. Leith has not studied the "Ritual of Ancient Egypt," because the Pyramid is part of the Ritual written in Stone. Therein he will find a definite answer and solution to all his questions. The two books he quotes are perverted parts of this ancient book, the oldest in the world. "The Secret Doctrine of Madame Blavatsky" shows a small amount of knowledge—gained principally, I believe, in India —of this Ritual, mixed with a great many errors and hypothetical ideas which, critically, must fall to the ground. She uses terminology she cannot understand, which without the interpretation from the Ritual has no meaning. I give an example, which is sufficient, although a dozen might be taken :—

" Listen ye Sons of the Earth to your instructors, the Sons of the Fire, learn there is neither First nor Last, for All is One Number issued from No Number. Learn what we, who descend from the Primordial Seven, we who are born of the Primordial Flame, have learned from our fathers. From the effulgency of light the ray of ever-darkness sprang in space the re-awakened energies. The one from the egg, the six and the five. Then the three, the one the four, the one the five, the twice seven, the sum total. And these are the Flames, the Essences, the Builders, the Force, the Divine Man."

In the Egyptian representation there are seven Souls of life-forces recognized in nature. Six of these were pre-human—elementary forces or powers born of the Primary Great Mother, when there was yet no human soul distinguished from the six that were souls, such as light or air, earth or water, and animal or vegetable life. The seventh Soul was human. This was the Soul of Blood, brought forth by a goddess in the human likeness. The Blood Mother was imaged by the Virgin Neith (see " Signs and Symbols of Primordial Man "). These six were pre-anthropomorphic, the seventh was human, $6 + 1 = 7$. They were the elementary children of the Great Mother, six Brothers and One the leader, or Great One of the company. Sut, the male Hippopotamus ; Sebek, the Crocodile ; Shu, the Lion ; Hapi, the Ape ; Anup, the Jackal ; Kabhsenuf, the Hawk ; and One the Elder Horus, the Human, as The Chief. This was the same in Totemism and the mythology, and all descended from the Great Mother, who was mythical.

The change in the human descent from the motherhood to the fatherhood is not apparent in the mythology until the time of Ptah, the father of Atum-Ra, but these seven were carried on from their Totemism and Mythology to the Stellar Mythos, and from the Stellar to the Lunar, then to the Solar, and finally are brought on in the Eschatology in different forms and characters, and in the present day are represented both in the Hebrew and the Christian doctrines in various forms.   It is in Atum-Ra, or Tum, who was both male and female, that we find "one all Parent."   In the Ritual, ch. xvii., Tum is described as giving birth to Hu and Sa as the children of him who now unites the Father and Mother as divinity in one person.   Hu denotes matter, Sa or Ka signifies spirit.   This creation then is from blood and spirit, "the double primordial essence" first assigned to Ptah.

These were the seven Souls or elementary powers represented by Zootypes, in the primary form, and were the primordial forms of the primary powers that were derived at first from the Mother

Earth and the elements in external nature, and
these gods became astronomical or astral, as the
Khus or Glorious Ones in the Celestial Hepta-
nomes of Heaven in seven divisions.   In Stellar
Mythos (at the time of the building of the Great
Pyramid) they became the seven Glorious Ones,
seven Pole Stars (Ursa Minor), whom we read of
in the Ritual (ch. xvii), who were the seven with

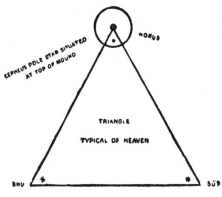

FIG. 17.

Horus in Orion, seven with Anup at the Pole of
Heaven, seven with Taht, seven with Ptah, and
finally with Ra and Osiris as the seven Gods of
Eternity.   The three represented, Sut, Shu, and
Horus (see Fig. 17), formed the primary Trinity
and the primordial Triangle ; Horus situated at the
North Pole Star ; Sut at the South, and Shu at
the Equinox.   This was represented as the Triangle

7

of Heaven, and was typified by the door of Pyramid, which was a triangular stone revolving on its axis (see " Signs and Symbols of Primordial Man "). The one and the four. The one was Horus—the four were the four brothers of Horus, afterwards called the children of Horus, who were the four supports of Heaven when this was represented by the Square—and here in the Pyramid symbolized by the four stones, which form a square over the entrance. The " flame born of a flame " was Horus, the child of Hathor, who came forth at dawn as the Young Sun God. Hathor, the Moon Goddess, descends into the underworld, and there meets the Sun, and obtains regeneration of Light from the Sun (Lunar mythology). In Ritual, ch. xvi., it is stated : " Thou art Horus, the Son of Hathor, the flame born of a flame." Here Horus is born and is represented as the Child of Light, who became in the Eschatology the Divine Man.

" The one from the Egg ! " How would Madame Blavatsky have rendered the meaning of this mystery? Yet in the Ritual it is plain. The God of the Earth was Seb, whose Zootype in the mythology was a Goose that laid the Egg. Now the Egg that was laid was the Sun setting in the West, which was " hatched out " in the underworld and came forth in the East as the Young Sun—" Giver of Light," etc.—and was typical of

Horus, the Young Sun God. Her book is a mixture of a little of all the Mythologies and Eschatology jumbled together, and has no meaning without the interpretation of the Ritual of Egypt.

The Second Pyramid (one of three) was built to memorize Sut. "The Pyramid of Sut, when Sut was the first. The God of the Pole Star South, El Shaddai." How long Sut reigned as God of the South it is impossible to state, but that he did so for many thousands of years there is ample proof still extant. It was known by these old wise men of Egypt that as they travelled North from their original homes—Equatorial Provinces—Sut would go down and disappear in the underworld, and that Horus (North Polar Star) would rise in the ascendant and be permanently established for ever. Hence the changes, first from Sut being a primary God, second as a brother to Horus, and third, that "he descended" as Horus "ascended." He then became the type of the Great Evil One in one form, and Ap-Uat, a form of Set-Anup, in another, the guider of the way of the underworld. This is written and symbolized in the Second Pyramid. It is also symbolized as the change from the worship of El Shaddai (Phœnician name of Sut) to the worship of Ihuh, Hu or Iu Eu, and corresponds to the change from the Eloistic to the Jehovistic God, which was the change from the Stellar to the Solar Mythos (1 Chron. xii. 5).

As regards age, the Pyramids were erected at the earliest time of these astronomical observations, at the time that Sut (El Shaddai) was the supreme God of the South, situated at the South Pole Star. He was always represented as *red*, and the Arabs have a tradition that this was the burial-place of Sut—but of course Sut was mythical, only a type, and represented night or darkness after. The Pillar of Red Brick, being less permanent, went down as predicted in the deluge as a figure of the Southern Pole, whereas the Pillar of Stone (North Great Pyramid) remained for ever as an image of the Celestial Pole, or of Annu, the Site of the Pillar, in their astronomical mythology. It was reported by Diodorus that Annu (Heliopolis in the Solar Mythos) was accounted by its inhabitants to be the oldest city in Egypt, which may have been mythically meant, as Annu was also a city or station of the Pole, the most ancient foundation in the northern heaven, described in the Eschatology as a place of a thousand fortresses provisioned for eternity. The two pillars of Sut and Horus were primal as pillars of the two Poles, thus figured in the equatorial regions as the two supports of heaven, when it was first divided into two portions, South and North, and the pillar or mount of the South was given to Sut, and the pillar of the North to Horus. The typical two pillars are identified with and *as* Sut and Horus, in the inscription of Shabaka from Memphis, in which it is said, "*The two pillars of the gateway of the House of Ptah are Horus and Sut.*" Thus the two pillars at the entrance are explained. The great stones built into the masonry, and fourfold, set with a Triangular Stone, which acted on its pivot for providing an entrance, is symbolical of Heaven and Earth. The four supports of Heaven, when Heaven was represented as a Square, and this Earth was also depicted as a Square. The Triangle was the sacred Triangle of Sut, Horus, and Shu, and represented the original Trinity in its earliest form. The passing through this door was symbolical of passing from Earth to Heaven (see " Signs and Symbols of Primordial Man "). It is only by the Ritual that you can decipher the meaning and unlock the hidden mystery of the past, here written in stone. If students will learn Stellar Mythos and read the Ritual of Ancient Egypt, they will have no doubt left as to the origin and meaning of it all ; it is the key of the wisdom of the old Egyptic Theopneustics, left for future generations to read and learn after a dark and degenerate age. I have written " Signs and Symbols of Primordial Man " for all those Brothers who cannot obtain the Ritual, or, if obtained, cannot read it.

The "Star Sothis" was "The Star of the White Spirits," i.e. it was the place where all the white spirits came forth after travelling through the underworld in the earliest time of the Egyptian Mythology, during their totemic sociological state, and during the time of Stellar Mythos—before Amenta was formed, and therefore pre-Solar. In Stellar Mythos it was the Star of Annunciation, it heralded the birth of Horus. It was the Morning Star of the Egyptian year—365¼ days—and their Great Year—25,827 years. In Lunar Mythos it was the Star of Hathor and her infant son Horus, and above all to these oldest observers it was the herald of the Inundation, telling them when the Nile would come down and fertilize the land, and food would be plentiful as a good result of inundation. Most important and sacred rites were connected with the rising of this Star, which we need not enter into here. *But here was within the Great Pyramid the time of the commencement of the New Year which was the commencement of the Precession of the seven Pole Stars (Ursa Minor), ending with the seventh Pole Star Hercules, " The Man "—the* $6 + 1 = 7$. The six periods of the world's existence, ending with the seventh, taking 25,827 years to perform.

To recommence again : *To begin another Great Year and not to be swallowed up in Eternity when time shall be no more.* This time of reckoning was carried from Egypt by the Stellar Mythos people throughout the world, as witnessed by the Glyphs on the Ruins at Copan and Palanque and in Peru amongst the Aymaras.

That Sut or Set was first primary god of the Egyptians, but was god of the South Pole, or Southern Hemisphere, is amply proved and borne out by the monuments as well as the Ritual. Set or Sut, according to Plutarch, is the Egyptian name of Typhon—i.e. Satan of the Christian Cult. On the oldest monuments it has been almost invariably chiselled out ; we find the names of kings who have taken his name, in the same manner as we afterwards find the Horus name. And although the legend of the conflict between Horus and Sut is as old as the Fourth Dynasty at least, it is, however, likewise a proof of Set's position having once been very different. It is he whose sign is changed for that of Osiris in the letters of the Father of the Great Rameses, and two other kings of that Dynasty ; it is the same god with his ordinary monumental name, Nubi (in Nubian), who is pouring out life and power over the King. His hierographic figure of a giraffe is the Nubian primary god Set, or Sut, and with Anup added the translation is : " The Lord of the Southern Hemisphere," as witnessed in the temples and monuments of Karnak and Medinet Habu. The first figure here to remark is Horus (Amun-Khem) to whom the

King is sacrificing and doing homage, and Horus
is pouring out life and power over the King. The
fact that we find Sut here as one of the great Gods,
is a proof that he was considered and looked upon
at the earliest period of their mythology as at least
a brother to Horus, and that now Horus was
primary. The myth had shifted, or changed
places, the domain of Paradise from the South to
the North, and the great fight between Horus and
Sut had not yet come into being. There can be no
doubt that the primary part of the Mythos was first
evolved at the Lakes at the head of the Nile when
the Southern Pole Star was most predominant.
The different names of Set taken by Kings which
we find on the oldest monuments, some of which
have been obliterated and Horus and Osiris substituted, prove this, as well as the Pyramids and
the Ritual. On later monuments we find that the
great contest had been worked out in their mythology, and his name is then found Apap (the
Great Giant, the Great Evil Serpent). In the
Book of the Ritual he is also called Baba—the
Beast [(ch. xc. 17, 66, 67)—and the struggle of
Horus and Sut is mentioned in the Ritual (ch. viii.
17, 9, 25), "The day of battle between Horus
and Sut." Thus these old forefathers of ours had
first worked out their Paradise in the Southern
Hemisphere, and then as they came North, and a
general amalgamation of the attributes took place,

it was transferred to the Northern in the type of Horus, Lord of the Northern Heavens. The above, we think, will explain the reason of the building of the "Southern Pyramid." It might be of interest to know that there was *only one known inscribed stone in the Great Pyramid. It was at the South.* Mr. Don Covington discovered this "let-in-stone," clearly incised in the dressed surface. It was the full tenth part of an eighteen-inch diameter circle ; it had been let into a south flank casing stone at a place from which another inscription had been chiselled out. This shows that the Pyramid was built at the early part of the Stellar Mythos with the hieroglyphic for the King of the Southern Hemisphere, and when the change took place to the Lunar and Solar this was erased and the Lunar and Solar sign substituted.

The Pyramids were built during the Stellar Mythos, when the old wise men of Egypt had worked out the Astral Mythology, which was then carried all over the world. This is witnessed by the ancient remains, huge and magnificent buildings once which flourished in a high state of civilization, and critically proven by the similarity of the build-ings, identical Signs and Symbols, and fragments of ancient writings, Egyptian hieroglyphics, which can only be deciphered now by the wisdom of old Egypt. The exodus, which we may class under the name of the early Turanians, occurred some six hundred thousand years ago, probably much more, because we have still the colossal wrecks of wonderful empires which stand to-day, pitiful monuments to the greatness of the builders and the everlasting shame of the men who accomplished their ruin.[1] The Titanic monuments of a forgotten past found in Central and South America, and some parts of Asia, like the African ruins of Zimbabwi, the Great Pyramids, lead most men to exclaim, " Who were these old builders? Whence came they? By what lost art did they chisel those perfect edges and angles? By what means did they move these ponderous masses to such perfect adjustment, a marvel of delicate and beautiful workmanship? Overwhelming in their grandeur are those scattered remains." It is only by the origin and evolution of man that an irrefutable answer can be given. They came from Egypt, and their Temples and buildings can always be identified. These Stellar people always built iconographically. The Solar did not because the gods and goddesses which had been represented by Zootypes in the Stellar cult were now (in the Solar) represented by the Human form. The Stellar therefore were prehuman and the Solar human depictions. They both built with Polygonal-shaped stones and Monoliths, but the Stellar works

[1] The same thing is being enacted again to-day by the German Huns,

can always be identified by their Iconographic forms.

The Pyramid is an artificial figure of the mount as a means of the ascent to heaven. The Initiate, placed at the bottom of the well, would see the tubular shaft of the Great Pyramid represented the way to heaven as it was imaged in Egyptian thought. Resting at the foot he could scan not merely the starry vast, but could fix his gaze in death upon the heaven of spirits at the summit of the mount, the Paradise of Peace, the enclosure that was finally configurated in the circle of the seven Pole Stars that crossed the passage pointing northward, one by one, in the circuit of precession, or the heaven of eternity. The Pole Star a Draconis was not the only one that would cross within range of that great tube. The Great Pyramid was founded on the Egyptian astronomy, but was not built to register the fact that a Draconis was the fixed point and polar pivot of all the Stellar motion during some 25,827 years in the vast circle of precession. The ceilings of the chambers were sprinkled with stars to resemble the sky by night (Maspero, " Dawn of Civilization "). Astronomical tables gave the aspect of the heavens, tenat by tenat, throughout the year, so that the Initiates " had but to lift their eyes " and see in what part of the firmament the course lay night after night. Thus he found his future destiny depicted thereon and learned to understand the blessings of the gods. The chief course was mapped out along the river of the Milky Way, as is shown in the Ritual by the boat of souls ascending to the Polar Paradise. The Initiate (who has been placed in the position of a mummy) now is risen up, and he is set in motion, prays that he may go up to Sekhet-Arru and arrive in Sekhet-Hetep. There are three forms of the boat of souls, one in the Stellar, one in the Lunar, and one in the Solar representation, at three different stages of the Mythos.

The Sun, Moon, and seven Stars are frequently grouped together on the Assyrian monuments. The Chinese call the Sun, Moon, and seven Stars the nine Lights of Heaven. The same grouping is observed in the nine Pyramids of the Mexicans —one for the Sun, one for the Moon, and seven small ones for the seven Stars. The three Pyramids of Gizeh answer to those of the Sun, Moon, and seven Stars elsewhere. The Great Pyramid is in itself a sign of seven, comprising, as it does, the Square and the Triangle in one figure. Its name, Khuti, means also the Seven Glorious Ones, as well as Light. It was designed by the Har-seshu, or servants of Horus, who were the seven Khuti in the Stellar Mythology ; they had been the rulers in the celestial hepta-nomes before they became the seven servants of the Solar God. The seven periods of the Pole Stars were also imaged by seven Eyes, in consequence of an Eye being the figure of a cycle. This type is presented in Joshua, in the book of Zechariah, in the shape of seven eyes on one stone ; " Behold the stone that I have laid before Joshua ; upon one stone are seven Eyes." These are the seven Eyes of the Lord ; also the seven Lamps ; as in Revelation.

But to write the whole explanation and interpretation even of these seven would form a book of many pages. My object is more to draw attention to two books which will give, I think, all the explanation and interpretation desired, viz. " The Ritual of Ancient Egypt," published by the Trustees of the British Museum, which gives a facsimile of all the Papyri, as well as the text of the same in hieroglyphics, or, if one cannot read the Egyptian hieroglyphics, Sir Le Page Renouf's translation. The other book is " Signs and Symbols of Primordial Man."

In his second article Mr. F. E. Leith has fallen into an error, important to correct, because it is " The Ritual of Resurrection," or so-called " Book of the Dead," to which I referred, and not to Mr. Marsham Adams' book.

I do not intend to criticize Mr. Leith's writings because he has evidently spent a great deal of time and study in trying to obtain the hidden

secrets of this Great Building, and his decipherments, taken as a whole, are not far from correct,
and the errors contained therein are due to the
fact that he has not sufficiently studied " The
Ritual of Resurrection," the past history of the
world, and the origin and development of the
human race.

Another point is that he quotes Dr. Le Plongeon
as accepting the correctness of the " Book of
Dazan " for the explanation of the Pyramids and
Temples of the Maya.   Now, Dr. Le Plongeon
and his wife, Alice Le Plongeon, stayed with me
as my guests for a considerable time during the
writing of his works, and moreover he asked me to
read all his manuscripts before they were published.
This I did, and pointed out to him that he had
not differentiated between the Stellar and Solar
Temples, and had not taken into account any of
the previous Totemic people—which he acknowledged he did not understand.   But no one that
I know, or ever heard of before, took him as an
authority upon the above subject, though it is an
actual fact that he lived amongst the Mayas for
some time and discovered several ancient remains.
His deductions were, nevertheless, quite erroneous.
In the first place, he did not know the Egyptian
language, or even Hindoo, or Zend ; and although
he tried to compare the Egyptian Hieroglyphic
Alphabet and Ideographs with the Maya, he could

not, and did not, read the Egyptian correctly.
He accomplished great work by discovering many
ruins of Temples, etc., and obtained photographs
of the same, and deciphered the Maya characters
thereon.   There it ended.

Mr. Leigh quotes Herodotus, but Herodotus
only lived 484-424 B.C., and, moreover, was
ignorant of the Egyptian language, and had to
depend upon interpreters as to what was told him
by the Egyptian Priests.   He, however, made an
important statement connected with the Pyramid,
and that was : " *That Kufu (who was the supposed builder of the Pyramid) lived and reigned
in Egypt during the Solar Mythos, but that Kufu
was not the builder*."   Now we know, for a fact,
that the recent discoveries at Abydos prove that
this cult (Solar) was at its zenith there twenty
thousand to thirty thousand years ago, and at Heliopolis, before that, more than eighteen thousand
years before the time of Moses.   Now as regards
the time, and who were the builders of the Pyramid,
we have a very definite fact by the greatest and
oldest Egyptian historian, Manetho, who was a
high priest and kept " The Records of Egypt."
His statement is that the Great Pyramid was built
at the end of the reign of " The Gods and the
Heroes "—that is, at the time when their Totemic
Sociology had arrived by evolution in the Stellar
Mythos—" and it was built by the followers of

Horus." Moreover, he states that "the Gods and Heroes" were not human, nor ever had been human. The followers of Horus were the Stellar Mythos people in the same sense as Christians are the followers of Christ.

I have proved (and this proof has now been accepted by the greatest anthropologists and ethnologists) that the human race sprang from Africa, and not Asia. It was there in old Africa that man began to develop his faculties and spread all over the world, taking with him, at various epochs, all the knowledge at the time of the exodus with which he left. The first were the Pygmies, with no Totemic ceremonies, but with a belief in a Great Spirit and a Spiritual life hereafter, and with a propitiation of elemental powers. The second were the Nilotic Negroes, with Totemic ceremonies, and a later exodus of these, when the elemental powers became divinized. Then the Stellar Mythos people, in at least two if not three different stages of evolution. After these the Lunar and then the Solar people, and finally the Christian doctrine was evolved, and is now spreading and replacing all previous cults.

But the Stellar Mythos people, whose cult lasted three hundred thousand years at least, as witnessed and proved by the Ritual, "They covered up my eye after them with bushes (or hairy net) twice, for ten periods" (a period being one Great Year,

25,827 years, or one revolution of the Little Bear or precession of the Pole Stars), had reached the highest stage of evolution eschatologically and astronomically, which stage has never been surpassed ; they were the greatest of all.   It was these people who built the Great Pyramids in Egypt, Central and South America, and other parts of the world where we now find the remains, and had then finally developed the whole of the present eschatology.   Mr. Leith is wrong in trying to bring a Biblical proof for the whole of his contention. It cannot be done as an exoteric rendering.   Can he or any one else bring forward any proof of the history?   No ; for there was no history as an exoteric rendering.   The oldest authorities that we have, and all their writings which are extant, prove this.   And here let me state also that Mr. Leith is absolutely wrong in attributing " The Dazan " as the oldest book in the world.   " The Ritual of the Resurrection of the Egyptians " is the oldest.   But the Biblical wisdom, as an esoteric rendering, or, rather, representation of the Ritual of Ancient Egypt, is true, and all can be read and understood.   Geology, and the remains of skeletons of the human found in various places, prove that man has existed here on this earth at least one million years.   A skeleton of a man found in a coal bed in America, and one found in Germany 87 feet below the surface, the bed of which was formed by running water, as well as the Sussex human found in this country, is sufficient proof that Biblical dates cannot be taken as correct.

The Great Pyramid was built during the Stellar Mythos. In it is portrayed the whole architecture of the heavens, courses and times of the heavenly bodies, the seasons of the year, days of the year and Great Year, time measurements and distance of the sun and moon and their time of revolution, as well as the Pole Stars. The whole of their eschatology is there written for all those who can read, and for a witness from all time since it was built, when the man-god Horus was slain and rose again as Amsu in spirit form, until all the world will be re-united again under one divine brother-hood.

I have written this in a broad sense, as I feel it will be taken in a more fraternal spirit than if I had taken each of the points put forward, and disproved many by historical records of the past. I think Mr. Leith's articles very interesting, and most of his structural ideas regarding the Pyramid are quite correct ; this I know from personal visits. But for the rest—the authorities he quotes neither knew the Egyptian language nor the Zend, which was, and is that which followed the Ancient Egyptian, not the hieroglyphic, the oldest, but the hieratic. The Zend is the oldest extant sacred writings in Asia, as the sacred books exist amongst some of the priests in India and elsewhere. Capt. Charles Serres, many years ago, brought me back one of these " sacred Bibles " from the Burmah priests ; it was written in the old Zend on flattened pieces of bamboo, about two feet long and three inches wide. The whole work is a copy of some parts of the Ritual of Egypt somewhat perverted. I am of the same opinion as Mr. Leith, that in future years—at the time of the next glacial epoch—Egypt will be the centre of civilization again, and all those lands and people of the Sumarians, Assyrians, Babylonians, Persians, Greeks, and Romans, which nations rose and fell in the above order, will rise again and a fraternal bond will unite them with their " old mother home." But it will not be until these islands are covered with glacial ice and snow, when the whole Northern human race is driven South again, as far as latitude 56 (as it had been many times before). Then, after the glacial epoch has passed away, the remains of the present humans, and their works, will be rediscovered by a future generation. What Great Masonic Temple will be left to the world? The first and greatest of all— The Great Pyramid of Egypt.

IV

THE DIVINE NAME

THE Rev. Jacob E. Warren, in an article on the above subject, asks for the origin of the "Divine Name" which the Hebrew text gives as Yhvh, and what we can do to discover the lost treasure? The answer is simple—study this question : Where did the Hebrews obtain it from?

The origin of the divine name above is from the

FIG. 18.    FIG. 19.

Egyptian Hu (Fig. 18) and Iu (Fig. 19), one of the names of Horus. This is the name " for the word," although there is still another secret name only known to a few which I am not permitted to divulge ; but the meaning of the words in each case is identical. The Hebrews obtained all their knowledge from the Egyptians, and to understand the Volume of the Sacred Law it must be read as an esoteric representation, and not an exoteric rendering.   Most people do the latter, which is terribly misleading for those who are ignorant of the ancient Egyptian wisdom.   Hu=Iu, signifies in Egyptian The Lord of the Heavens and the Earth—ruler of the destiny of the world. The original word was written Hu, then Iu, Iau, Iahe, as the son of Hu, which two were one.

In later times the letter I was changed into Y, which students would do well to bear in mind in trying to decipher names as written at the present day.   The letter Y did not exist until many, thousands of years after the letter I had been formed.   Another form for the name was Heru-Khuti=Light of the World.

The Jews used the word Iah—Jehovah ; Phœnicians, Iao ; Hebrew, Iah ; Assyrian, Iau ; Egyptian-gnostic, Ieou ; Polynesian, Iho-Iho ; Dyak, Yavuah or Iaouh ; Nicobar Islands, Eewu ; Mexican, Ao ; Toda, Au ; Hungarian, Iao ; Manx, Iee ; Cornish, Iau ; Welsh, Iau ; Chaldean, Iao-Heptaktes ; Greek, Ia and Ie.   The Jews were originally the followers of Aiu or Iu or Iau.   The worshippers of Iao in Phœnicia, of Iau in Assyria, of Iao in Syria, Iau and Hu in Britain, Ia or Iu in Greece, Iho-Iho in Polynesia, Iau in America, were each and all of them " Jews," in a sense, but the sense was religious, not originally ethnical.   *It was part of the Solar doctrines or Eschatology of the Egyptians.* The Dyaks of Borneo did not obtain their *Yavuah* from the Hebrew Jehovah, but from the origin of both.

The change in Israel from the worship of El Shaddai to the worship of Ihuh (=Hu or Iu in Egypt), from the Eloistic to the Jehovistic God, corresponds to the change from the Stellar to the Solar doctrines in the Eschatology of the Egyptians, which can be seen and proved in the Volume of the Sacred Law—in the book of 1 Chronicles xii. 5, in which we find that Baal-Jah, as divinity, supplied a personal name. Thus the Baal is Jah, who is one of the Baalim, the Primary or Superior one of the seven Stellar attributes. The one God in Israel was made known to Moses by the two names of Ihuh and Iah. In the Egyptian the one God in the earliest Solar form was *Tum*— (the earliest form of Atum-Ra)—he was Huhi, the eternal, in the character of God the Father, and Iu or *Tem*, in the character of God the Son, which two were one.

Gesenius derives the name Ihuh, or later Yhuh, from the root Huh, which root does not exist in Hebrew, but it does exist in Egyptian. Huh or Heh signifies ever, everlastingness, eternity, the eternal, and was one of the titles associated or names of Horus. The names changed from Tum, Ptah, Atum-Ra, Osiris, as Neb-Hui, the Ever-

lasting Lord, or Superior One ; Self-existing and
Eternal God, which each of the above represented
in turn, as one divine dynasty succeeded another
in the Egyptian Religion.

Moreover, Bela Baal was El Shaddai of the
Phœnicians, or was another name for him, and
when they changed from the Stellar (represented
by Sut-Anup) to Horus he was no longer to be
considered the one God (see Exodus xxxiv. 13).
" Thou shalt call me Ishi, and shalt call me no
more Baali " (Hosea ii. 16), and therefore to have
the Hebrew character of El Shaddai (or Phœnician
rather) as the Father, and Hu—Iu, Iau, Ishi, Ihu,
etc., as his Son, as is represented on our Cross of
the 18°, is quite wrong ; it has no meaning, and
no explanation could be given that would be correct
with the Hebrew characters on the symbol as it is
now ; but if these were changed to the Egyptian
(Fig. 18), or the equivalent, it would be correct,
would correspond, and have the same meaning
as Yhuh.

El Shaddai was not " a form of Father " to Hu
or Iu in any way.   He was the *Primary God
situated at the Southern Pole*, or hemisphere, for
upwards of fifty-one thousand years, and then he
was deposed in favour of Horus, the God of the
Northern Horizon.   This is proved by the two
Great Pyramids of Ghizeh, one built for Sut and
the other for Horus ; their names are inscribed

thereon ; it is clearly mentioned several times in the Egyptian Ritual. All the attributes hitherto associated with Set of the South were appropriated and given to Horus of the North, and this Cult lasted at least three hundred thousand years.

This Deity as the God of Israel was Jashal-El ; the God of Jashar-Ieshurun or Baali ; and the other forms of the name, El-Eloun, Edoni (Phœnician) at first, then changing, with the changing of the Stellar to the Solar Cult or Eschatology of Egypt. This gives the answer to the question.

The jealousies of the different sects of Christianity have led to a display of bitterness and hatred which have been the means of alienating thousands who believe that brotherly love and charity should be the principles of Christianity. Yet all these various denominations work under the banner of Christianity. The Church must obliterate its schisms, and if the Brotherhood of Freemasonry helps it to do so, then well indeed will it be. One looks back with horror to the days not long passed when men were burnt and tortured to the honour and glory of God under the name of Christianity. The Church must get rid and free itself from its despotism, its lack of that great virtue, Charity, and its badly-concealed hatred of all who have differed from its dogmas.

Until this has been really accomplished it will

be quite vain to expect churches to imitate the examples of our Lodges and "be penetrated through and through" with our great principles. Amongst the Ancient World the principles and tenets of our Brotherhood, the highest principles of Morality, Charity, Truth, and Justice, were practised by all, over three hundred thousand years ago, and such perfection was reached that our old Brothers would blush with shame to see us at the present time.

V

THE SECOND CENTURY OF MODERN MASONRY !

IT is a great pity we have so few students in Freemasonry who take an interest in the real history of our Brotherhood ; and still more to be deplored that there is no encouragement for those that do ; but if Masons would only search and read the records of the past they would never have fallen into the error and published the theory *that we were once operative masons:* and when I read in *The Freemason,* July 22, 1911, " The celebration in 1917 of the two-hundredth anniversary of Speculative Masonry which succeeded operative masonry in 17,17," it pained me to feel that this want of knowledge throughout the Universal Masonic Fraternity is one of the causes why some have wandered from the Cradle of their Home.

No doubt this idea was taken from Krause, who has endeavoured to prove that Masonry originated in the associations of operative masons that in the Middle Ages travelled through Europe. At best these " operatives " could only be carriers, or a connecting link of the Middle Ages and the Mysteries of the Ancient Egyptians. Likewise were the Greeks, who obtained their knowledge partly through the Pelasgians and Samothracia, and partly through a few of the best-informed Greeks, who went to Egypt and were initiated there into the lesser Mysteries by the Egyptian Priests.

Mr. Harold Bayley, in his " A New Light on the Renaissance," has shown and proved, by the various groups of signs and symbols which he has brought together, how, after the downfall of the Egyptian Empire, these sacred Egyptian signs and symbols were in one way brought on by the early Christians, and shown how some were converted into our present ones, and how a remnant of these men who possessed and clung to the true doctrines survived, and what they had to endure from the bigoted and ignorant early Roman Priests, who, ignorant of the true Eschatology, tried to, and did to a great extent for some time, usurp the temporal power by destroying the spiritual ideas ; however, evolution has always, and still continues, its course to a higher standard. But we do not need even " these carriers " in England for the origin of our Brotherhood here.

It is impossible to say if it took the form of

" Craft Masonry " first in England or Scotland.
The word Freemason is met with in MS. as far
back as A.D. 1376. The oldest Lodge record is
that of the Aitcheson Lodge, date 1598 ; that is
one year older than No. 1 Lodge of Edinburgh,
1599.

The Druids were first persecuted and driven
to secret meetings in England, as may be seen
from Canute's edict ; but that is immaterial, and
I only mention it because the Scotch people
claim to be " the oldest Masons." Certainly some
of the " carriers " came to Scotland, as is
proved by research, but it is questionable if they
brought over any fresh or newer developments
in the Egyptian Eschatology—this they already
found here.   Bro. Gould, to whom we are much
indebted for the beautiful work he has given to
the Brotherhood, dealing with the modern and
historic aspect of Freemasonry from a later date,
I believe differs somewhat in his views from mine,
but I have not the slightest doubt, if he could read
the old dead and primary written languages, he
would modify his opinion.

If Masonry has not its origin in the Sacred
Mysteries of the Ancient Egyptians, how could
these rites and ceremonies, signs and symbols, have
found their way into it?   These sacred mysteries
were the same amongst the Priests of the Mayas
in Central America and Peru in South America.

The passwords for the various degrees are the same, or have the same meaning ; the signs and symbols are the same ; and the Rituals are identical ; which can be proved by any Brother who will take the trouble to learn to read the old hieroglyphic languages. I shall be glad, for the sake of the Brotherhood generally, when the intellectual aspects of Masonry have advanced many degrees beyond what they are now ; but this will, and can only, be done by *persistent individual labour and effort*, for the good of the Brotherhood generally, with no reward except the gratitude we shall receive from our children's children when our spirit has joined the Grand Lodge Above.

VI

SOME SUBJECTS SUGGESTED FOR STUDY

A Lecture delivered before the Essex Masters' Lodge, No. 3256, at the Great Eastern Hotel, London, E.C., on the 1st April, 1912.

FOR the last twenty years it has been one of my objects in life to give Brothers information and to assist in advancing Freemasonry to that position it occupied at least three hundred thousand years ago—and towards which we are now fast approaching. It was difficult for me to choose which particular subject would be most interesting to you, and I took my key from your W.M.'s letter saying that "you did not initiate," and therefore presumed you were students of Freemasonry.

Recent history has been so ably debated and written upon by many other students of Freemasonry that they have practically exhausted the subject. At this stage it is as if the students stood on the edge of the sea—let us say at Dover : some would stand wondering what was on the opposite side of the water, wishing to cross and see, but, having no boats and being unable to swim, would be brought to a standstill ; others would say that there was nothing across the water, while yet again some few, having caught sight of the white cliffs of France, would feel certain that there must be a great land there, but lack the key which would transport them thither. It is the same with Freemasonry, the Recent History being separated from the mysteries of the past by a gulf. How, then, is one to unlock these mysteries?

By one way only, and that is to learn to read the old Hieroglyphic writings of Egypt, and the Glyphs of the old Stellar Mythos people (or a translation), who worked out the whole of the Eschatology and left records of the same written in stone and on Papyri—in Signs and Symbols and in Sign Language, and if you do not read these you can never obtain that which many of you are striving to understand. From the downfall of the old Egyptian Empire, five thousand years ago, or more, up to the last few hundred years, we have passed through a dark and degenerate age. Then our altars were thrown down, our Brotherhood scattered over the face of the earth, and some of our secrets were lost to many. But there were remnants of the Brotherhood who went forth from Egypt into various parts of the world, carrying the true doctrines and secrets with them, some one part, some another.

Also there were the Druids, the old High Priests of Egypt, the Solar Mythos people, i.e. those who reckoned time by the Sun's revolutions, who were initiated up to the 33°, practising all their rites and ceremonies in France, in Central America, and in these islands, until the edict of Canute scattered them here, and forced them to meet in secret places —on the highest hill, or in the lowest vale, or any other secret place, the better to guard against cowans and enemies. Also in America their altars were thrown down, their Blazing Star was eclipsed. All was given over to fire and sword. The remains of their greatness still exist, to the everlasting shame of their destroyers. But if you look for any regular written history of the Order, you will not find it. There are no records left to us— but you may take it that from that time the so-called Lodges in England and Scotland were formed by a scattered few, who, to avoid the terrors of the law, and to keep their religious rites and ceremonies pure and unsullied, as they had received them from the parent source—old Egypt—met in secret places and had resort to private meetings. This, therefore, was one original source. There were no records left, in these islands, any more than there will be after another twenty thousand years have passed, or less

The Glacial Epoch occurs once in every 25,827 years, during part of which period the whole of the Northern Hemisphere is frozen and covered with ice and snow, down as far as the latitude of the south of France. This great City of London and others will be ground to pieces and buried underneath the Great Ice Sheet ; everything will be destroyed, as it has been many times ; only remains will be re-discovered by our future Brothers when they come North again, and who shall say how much or how little evidence will they then find of our present institutions and teachings?

As regards the Roman College of Artificers, Krause, in his work, endeavoured to prove that Masonry originated in the associations of operative Masons. These associations may have sprung from the building corporations of the Romans. The initiates of the Architectural Colleges of the Romans did not, however, call themselves " Brothers " ; they were styled Collega or Incorporatus. The Colleges held " Lodges " wherever they established themselves, had signs, symbols, tokens, and passwords, which they had learned and received from the Chaldean magicians, who flocked to Rome at the beginning of the Christian era. These Chaldean priests, nevertheless, were of inferior order, who were initiated into part of the lesser mysteries of the Egyptians only, so that at best these could only be carriers

9

or a connecting link in the Middle Ages with the Mysteries of the Ancients.

The "working or operative Masons"—and there are still many of these in existence—who use some of the primary signs and symbols of which we, as so-called "Speculative Masons," have substituted the modern forms, have a tradition that they came from the Turanians. Well, that is quite right and true. Some of the signs and symbols which they use are of a different form from ours, but the esoteric representation of each is the same —as, for instance, the Swastika (Tau and Cross), the meaning and explanation of which are all identical. These are innovations obtained from the Solar Cult people, and speaking truly did not belong originally to the operative. But they also say that the Egyptians came from the Turanians —which is quite wrong. These Chaldean magicians were Turanians, old Stellar Mythos people, who originally came out of or left Egypt at the end of their Totemic Sociology ; remnants of them are still found in various parts of the world, which they spread over, except Australia, Tasmania, Oceania, and extreme parts of South America. You will find positive proof of Egypt being the "home of man," from which all have taken their origin, in my "Origin and Evolution of Primitive Man."

By Stellar Mythos people I mean those who first

reckoned and kept time, and they did so by the observation of the Precession of the Pole Stars— Ursa Minor, or the Little Bear.   They did not reckon by the year, except the one great year of 25,827 years ; this they divided into periods, a period being roughly three thousand years—i.e. the changing of the Pole Star.   This Stellar period lasted over three hundred thousand years ; after which time was reckoned by the moon's revolutions, that was Lunar Mythos, and after that it was Solar, time being reckoned by the sun's revolutions, etc.

These Turanians had the Lesser Mysteries— the seven Primary Mysteries, and were astro-mythological.

The Greater Mysteries were ten in number, and were Eschatological and founded on the Mystery of the Cross.   This Mystery was the Great Mystery of Amenta, evolved at the foundation of the Solar Cult, over thirty thousand years ago. In the Solar Cult the two Poles I. I. North and South were converted into $+$ in Amenta.   Hence the reason that the Operative Masons and we Speculative Masons have only the Lesser Mysteries, up to the end of the seven, while in the so-called " Higher Degrees " they have some parts of the ten Greater Mysteries, and founded on the Cross established in Amenta.   Our primary Seven Degrees (so called) date back to the early

Stellar-Astro-Mythology, whilst the " Higher Degrees " are Eschatological and date back to the
commencement of the Solar Cult only.

Then as far as our Sacred Volume is concerned,
you must remember that not until Luther's time
did we have, speaking generally, any of these
exoteric writings to study, except a few extracts
given out by the Roman priests, and even then
the esoteric representations were not known, and
it is only during the last few hundred years that
we have kept written records of anything.

One might say that for five thousand years there
was no literature left us that we could read and
properly understand. The Greeks, who have been
much over-estimated, never understood the Eschatology, and, in their ignorance, perverted all that
had been told them ; and so it was not until a
few years ago that the discovery was made which
gave us the key to read the writings and to find
the true history of the past. The finding of various
Papyri with sacred writings, which we can now
read, proves what all our forms and ceremonies
meant, and from whence they came.

Here written on Papyri, on stones, and even on
the Great Pyramid itself, is our Ritual, with all
passwords, signs and symbols, and the meaning
of the same, and I, having discovered the key to
read the Central American Glyphs, which I have
now given to the rest of the world, found that

these writings and their Eschatology were copies of the Egyptian originals.

Freemasonry, taken as a whole, i.e. in all its degrees from first to thirty-third, is the Ritual of Ancient Egypt, or their Eschatology, i.e. the doctrine of final things, performed dramatically and symbolically, the more to impress it upon the initiates.

There are written records left in this old language, which I have read, and brought forward in my books, proving that this doctrine was extant and perfect, at least as long as three hundred thousand years ago. It teaches you the life you should lead here on earth to gain everlasting happiness. It portrays all the dangers and difficulties the Corpus has to pass through in this life, and the Manes in the next, to gain that glorious hereafter we are all striving to obtain.

Our present Ritual, Lodges, Passwords, etc., are not all identically the same as of old ; we have reconstructed at various times the secrets and parts of the Ritual as we have found them, and therefore there are necessarily innovations from the first to the thirty-third. Our M.M. Lodge is not correct in detail, but our R.A. Chapter is perfectly correct, and is a true copy of the Ancient Lodges, or Temples, of which we find the remnants, dating three hundred thousand years back, i.e. as nearly as possible considering time and evolution. The

18° Lodge is another that is nearly perfect, and was part of, or an attachment to, the first Temple or Lodge, their Temples consisting of three different rooms, or buildings, attached to one another and connected by doors and passages.

The three cubes, each one surmounting the other, formed one central pedestal, on top of which rested a circle of gold and a triangle—at the corners of this triangle were the names, in symbols, of the three names on the treble cube—namely, Horus, Set, and Shu, the first and Primary Trinity, and the three Grand Originals. Horus was typified and portrayed as the God of the North, Set as God of the South, and Shu as God of the Equinox. The triangle was sacred on account of its representing Heaven. The Primary Triangle originally represented Set, but when Horus took the place and attributes of Set, he became God of the Celestial North. Their two symbols were afterwards blended as Fig. 23. This form was sometimes doubled, as Fig. 20, and was then the most sacred sign amongst

the old Brotherhood ; an ideograph represented their " Khui Land," or " The Land of the Spirits," and we find it portrayed as such all over the

FIG. 20.

world, where the old Brothers had lived. This was, in Primary form, surrounded by four serpents or Uraei, as guardians of the same (Fig. 21) ; later it was three Triangles, doubled as above,

surrounded with concentric circles (Fig. 22). We
have it, as you know, surrounded with one circle.
I have in my possession what I believe to be the
oldest Scarab in the world with this sign on it,
at one time the jewel of the High Priest.   It
represents the two Triangles guarded by four
Uraei in front of the Scarab, and on the back an
Island in a Lake, the most sacred sign that ever
existed in our Brotherhood, and must date back
to the time of the High Priest of the seventeenth
nome of Upper Egypt at the time of Totemic

FIG. 21.

FIG. 22.

FIG. 23.

Sociology.   Because the " Khui Land " was " the
Land of the Spirits," i.e. Heaven, and was depicted as situated at the Pole Star North, i.e. this
Northern Land Paradise, surrounded by the waters
of space, and they portrayed and represented the
terrestrial by building a sacred temple on an island
in a lake.   Hence the reason we find the two
ideographs together, as in Fig. 23, one representing the Celestial and the other the Terrestrial.
You may ask, why two triangles?   It represents
symbolically—or is an ideograph of—Heaven in

two divisions, North and South, which was the primary heaven, being afterwards again divided into East and West, giving us the four quarters.

I do not know the password for the Grand Masters in England, but I do know the original sacred password of Old Egypt's Highest Priests. This word, which is given with and accompanies the above symbol, must only be communicated to, or spoken between, two Grand Masters, and never given to any one below that rank ; and I shall be pleased to restore the genuine sign, symbol, and passwords to any two Grand Masters if they so desire.

You will observe these are the two Triangles of Set and Horus.

The upper one, or North, is an ideograph for Horus.

The lower one, or South, that for Set.

The Heavens were first divided into two divisions, North and South, at the time of their Totemic Sociology—before the Stellar Cult—at the very earliest time of their Astro-Mythology.

The old Egyptians' custom was this : As they mapped out the Heavens Celestially, so they depicted the same Terrestrially in old Egypt. The North and South Pole Stars portrayed in the earliest form was by two Poles or two Columns, and this was an earlier phase than by the triangle. Amongst the Totemic people of the present day it

is still used in their sacred ceremonies. One pole
or column is placed North, and is called
Nurtunga, the other is placed South, and its
name is Warringa. As evolution took place and
Temples were built, these two columns were
brought on and placed at the entrance of all their
Temples, in whatever land they erected a Temple.
Their names all through the Stellar and Solar
Mythos were "Horus and Set," and represented
symbolically the God of the North and the God
of the South. You will find proof of this in
several chapters of the Ritual.

As evolution still progressed and when they had
perfected their Eschatology, the two columns still
continued to be placed at the entrance of their
Temples, only their names were changed to Tatt
and Tattu, and all Temples throughout the world
had these down to the time of the commencement
of the Christian cult. As you know, at the
entrance of our Temples we have the two columns ;
J and B are the names we use, but remember the
oldest names were Nurtunga and Warringa, and
that the later names, Tatt, which, in Egyptian,
means "In strength," and Tattu, which means, in
Egyptian, "To establish," denoting in Egyptian
the place of establishing for ever, were those from
which we copied them. So we learn how they
brought on and made use of the earliest originals,
and these have been handed down and made use

of from generation to generation to the present time ; the names changing, but not the esoteric symbolism.

The originals on the top of the two columns (see Fig. 15) were four lines, or cross sticks, i.e. heaven and earth, as a square, represented at the present day by the celestial and terrestrial globes. The Egyptians at this period, not understanding perspective, could only draw on the flat, and so had to represent the ideas and beliefs as shown. Later, they knew that the Earth was not square, nor yet flat, but its true form.

The Brothers were not called Freemasons then, but the operatives were called Craftsmen and Companions, as witnessed in Ritual, Ch. lxxx.   The term Companion dates back as far as Totemic Sociology, over three hundred thousand years ago. The Priests of these were the first originals of our Brotherhood.   The Companions in Egypt were a special and privileged body of Brothers who occupied the seventeenth nome of Upper Egypt, and these—and these alone—had certain special duties to perform connected with the Temples. The Chief of the Nome was the Head or High Priest, and he was the first original of our Grand Master. The Egyptian title was Ura-herp-Kem ; later a higher degree was formed, when his title was " The Most Illustrious," which means Master of Masters (Ritual, Ch. xiv.).   I note for your atten-

tion the Chapters in the Ritual where can be
found the origin and explanation for :

The desire for light	Ch. 9.
First Penal Sign	Ch. 90.
Heart torn out by fingers...	Ch. 27 & 28.
Body burnt to ashes, etc....	Ch. 86.
Given bread to the hungry	Ch. 125.
Left foot first—the Papyrus of Nesi-Amsu.	

These Sacred Mysteries were the same amongst
the priests of the Mayas, and in Central and
South America, the Druids, and the priests of
Egypt, and the same as we practise. The similarity of the rites practised in the initiation and
other ceremonies, the identity of the signs, symbols,
and tokens, proves that all these had been communicated from one to another, from one centre
of origin. Only in Old Egypt can we find that
origin ; it is all there.

And although in the so-called Higher Degrees
we have professedly Christian doctrines, yet any
Brother who will look at the reproduction (Fig. 1)
I have given of a picture, taken from an old Stellar
Mythos Temple, will see how little different is
the innovation at the present day. The so-called
Christian Cult which is the supposed latest in evolution is, in fact, the oldest. What I mean by
this is that the whole of the Christian doctrines
were the same as the original Stellar if you give

it the esoteric rendering. The same tale of the
Son of God coming on earth, being crucified, and
rising again is at least a million years old, and
all the different cults are one and the same
rendered esoterically. The dates of the V.S.L.
are wrong, but the tale is true.

If you wish to make progress as students of
Freemasonry you cannot ignore the history of the
evolution of the human race. It is only by learning this that you can gain that light which some,
I know, are striving to obtain. If you ignore
the history of the past you will still remain at the
seashore at Dover looking across the water, but
you will find other Brothers, in other countries,
racing across in steam-launches, or monoplanes, to
be the first to unite the broken ends of that cable-
tow which parted at the downfall of the old
Egyptian Empire. These ends are in your hands,
and in studying Freemasonry you must also study,
the origin and evolution of the human race. The
one is blended and evolved with the other, and
except you take the two together you will never
obtain the true gnosis.

There are many Freemasons who will scorn
these words, but they will do so from ignorance.
In fifty years' time these truths will be acknowledged as facts, because some of you will continue your studies, and will learn to read the
history of the past as I have, and it is only by

doing so that you can arrive at the Truth, the
Way, and the Light.

To those who are interested let me refer them
to " Signs and Symbols of Primordial Man " and
" The Origin and Evolution of Primitive Man,"
two works I have written for my Brother Masons
throughout the world, as well as many other
articles in Masonic journals, which will give you
more information on this subject, and guide you
into the true road of knowledge. I have written
them not for myself, but for Brothers throughout
the world, so that they may learn to know what
Freemasonry is—the origin, the truth, the real
meaning of it. It will elevate you then, for each
step which brings us back to our original is a
step of evolution towards the natural laws which
the Divine Creator has made. And so long as
we are true to our tenets and doctrines, believing
in the immutable laws of T.G.G. of the U., and
ever acknowledge Him as the Divine Creator
of all things, so long shall we continue to flourish.
We shall not have our altars thrown down again
and be scattered over the face of the earth, as
the Egyptians were on account of their falling
away from the true doctrines, as the records of the
past prove.

Evolution will not cease ; if one country degene-
rates and falls away, another country will arise
and go forward as a higher type. And so with

our Brotherhood, which is now approaching a
higher type of evolution rapidly, and will continue
to progress in a purer form.   A higher, nobler,
and more exalted conception will take the place
of Freemasonry that was here fifty years ago.   If
this country is broken up, and degeneration ensues,
or is absorbed into another nation, as others have
been before it, our Brotherhood will not fall with
it. It will be as it was once before—the Universal
religion and Brotherhood of the world.   Therefore
ever continue to seek after until you find the true
knowledge of the past, that will give you knowledge for the future, and enable you to exemplify,
by your every action, word, and thought, the most
exalted tenets of our Brotherhood, and by so doing,
and relying on the promises of the Most High,
the one Divine Creator of all things, we shall meet
again in that Grand Lodge above, where the reward
is Everlasting Life and Happiness.

VII

ORIGINS OF FREEMASONRY

A Lecture delivered before the Dorset Masters' Lodge No. 3366, at the Masonic Hall, Dorchester, on the 12th June, 1912.

As a Masonic student who has studied the history of the past ages more than, I believe, any other Mason living, I felt it would not only be a pleasure but a duty to try and assist in that great work for which this Lodge was founded. The difficulty on such an occasion as this is in selecting that subject, or subjects, which would be the most interesting and instructive, and as there are so many Brothers who write and lecture on the modern aspect of Freemasonry, I have thought it wiser to try and give a little more light upon the history of the past, so that you may be able to penetrate through that gloom of the darker ages, and be better enabled to appreciate what Freemasonry really is, in all its symbolisms, and to understand some of the workings of the Divine Creator's laws of evolution, and how we Freemasons are the privileged few who possess the originals in their true forms.

> The first question, then, is : What is Freemasonry?
>
> 2nd.   From whence did we derive our Signs, Symbols, and Rituals?
>
> 3rd.   What was the original meaning of our present interpretation and substituted difference?

Freemasonry in all its degrees, from the first to the thirty-third, is the old Eschatology of the Egyptians—or the doctrine of final things. We are divided at the present time into two classes —I might say three, if I include the "Operative Brothers." One class comprises the Master Mason, Mark Mason, and R.A.C., working the seven degrees of the old Stellar Mythos people, called the Lesser Mysteries—the seven mysteries worked out during the time they perfected their Astro-Mythology.

The second class, known as the higher degrees, under the Supreme Council, have part of, and work part of, the ten degrees of the Solar Mythos people—namely, the ten Greater Mysteries. To-day I am not entering upon any explanation of the latter ; they are not within the jurisdiction of this Lodge, and would probably only be of interest to some few of you. They are only an evolution of the former—i.e. as man advanced up the scale to a higher type, anatomically and physiologically, so his mental conception evolved a higher ideal of those sublime tenets which we are taught, and should practise.

Many students of Freemasonry at the present day have no doubt that all our Signs, Symbols, and Rituals have been handed down to us from generation to generation from the remotest past, but from whence they originated, and how it is that we are the greatest Brotherhood in the whole world—ever increasing in force, strength, and numbers, knit together in one bond—is a question that students ponder, and to which many are striving to obtain an insight. The casual Brother does not trouble his head about these things ; the majority look upon Freemasonry merely as a sort of Brotherhood for social intercourse and charity. Up to a certain point their views are correct ; our gatherings at the Lodges, and the social functions that follow after, tend to increase a fraternal feeling and goodfellowship one to the other. This is rightly so, and it is strengthened by the beautiful tenets and rituals which are taught and have been witnessed many times. As a charity it is certainly the greatest in the world, and we Freemasons are justly proud that it is, because each one gives according to his means, knowing that his gift is gratefully received and faithfully applied to the

10

good causes which come within the length of our C.T.

But there is a higher view. Freemasonry means much more than this. In Freemasonry we have many mysteries, handed down to us from remote ages, of a glorious past, a knowledge of which many are striving to obtain. This knowledge can be obtained only in one way, and that is by mastering the old writings of the Egyptians and glyphs of the Stellar Mythos people, or a transla- tion ; to obtain information of the evolution of man in all its phases, and to learn the history of the past, *because by that, and that alone, can the origin and meaning of all that is attached to the term " Brotherhood of Freemasonry " be found.*

But you must learn these; and not from ignorance, from the want of this knowledge, draw conclusions, make guesses, and theories, of what these ideographs, signs, and symbols are, as many writers on Freemasonry in the past and present have done—for instance, Bro. Armitage considers that the symbols found in ancient buildings were used by the building traders only ; in other words, by the Operative Masons. That is quite wrong, and this theory could only have arisen in the minds of those unable to read Sign Language. Bro. Gould has fallen into the same error.

The Mexican and Central American Glyphs and the Egyptian ideographic Signs and Symbols have the same interpretation, and, as I have often proved, all these are part of the Eschatology of the old Egyptians, and have nothing to do with the "Operative Masons," or Operative Masons' Marks, except indirectly. *The Operative Mason came into being at the time of building the Temples on their Astro-Mythological foundation.* These Operative Masons were initiated into some of the mysteries of the first and second degrees only, and were never advanced further in the old seven mysteries ; therefore you must not make the mistake about them that a great many have done, and still do, because they cannot read and understand Ancient Writings.

These are not Freemasons with the Ritual of old Egypt, with all their Eschatology, but were the builders of the Pyramids and Temples for the old High Priests, certainly three hundred thousand years ago or more. *The Priests of our cult, who were the learned men at that time, initiated a certain class of men into part of the first and second degrees, because the Great Pyramid and other Temples had to be built, and the secrets of these buildings kept.* These men came from the seventeenth Nome of Upper Egypt, and were descendants of the Madi, Nilotic Negroes. They were selected to be special attendants to the Temples, and were builders, etc., styled Companions and Craftsmen, in Egyptian. They always kept the secrets, and have ever done so, and I doubt very much if any Masons at the present day could erect such buildings as those old Turanians did.

This, I trust, will explain the differences between the Operative and Speculative Masons, and although many writers have mixed these up, the old Theopneustics of Egypt never did. There could be no such mixture there—they *knew*—the origin of the two being as I have stated. The proof of this can be found in the Ritual.

Our Brotherhood is the outcome of the evolution of religious ideas from the time of primitive man, who first adopted a sacred sign and symbol, propitiated the elementary powers, and believed in a Great Spirit, up to the period of the final working out and perfecting of the Eschatology (or doctrine of final things) of the Ancient Egyptians at their zenith of power. Obviously, however, much of the original must have been lost.   We have substituted our present innovations for that which we have lost—for instance, the genuine secrets of a M.M., which were the secrets of the underworld in the Stellar Mythos, and of Amenta in the Solar Cult.   The one, however, was only an evolution of the other.

The reason that we travel from East to West in search of that which is lost is that when Osiris lost his life by the machinations of Sut, like all

Manes he travelled from East to West to enter Amenta, and in the Stellar Cult travelled in the underworld.

Then in Amenta, after passing through difficulties, dangers, and darkness in the Tuat, his Manes was regenerated or raised again as Amsu-Horus, or Horus in Spirit, and he came forth from Amenta after entering the West to the Glorious Mount of the East again as a raised Manes or Glorified Spirit, and although this was Solar Cult, Ancient records prove that it was brought on from the Stellar. It is identical with the death of Horus I. and his rising again as Amsu in spirit form.

This was the origin of that part of the Ritual, for which we have substituted the name of H.A., who was not killed, but lived to a very old age. Proofs of this may be found in the V.S.L., Josephus, and others. (2 Chron. iv. 11 : " And Hiram finished the work that he was to make for King Solomon for the house of God." Josephus : " He lived at Tyre long afterwards.")

Isis and Nephthys tried first to raise him, but it proved a failure ; then Anubis raised him, as at present carried out. It was not the body Corpus that was raised, but the Spiritual body, or Sahu, that was raised up out of the dead matter Corpus. He returned to the East with all the secrets of Amenta. That is the true and original answer to

the question of What is that which was lost?
*The secrets of Amenta, or the underworld, were
the genuine secrets of a M.M.*

The genuine password for a Master of the Lodge
in Egypt is " Maat Heru," one whose voice must
be obeyed.   Here it was, in Amenta, that the Tatt
Cross was thrown down ; here it was that the veil
of the Temple was rent asunder, and the Cubic
Stone poured forth blood and water, and all was
reborn.   Here he was shown all the signs, given
and taught those passwords, or words of power
and might that kept evil and powers of darkness
away, and enabled him to pass through the underworld and be raised to the glorious resurrection in
Spirit form.   The Egyptian religion, which was
universal throughout the world at one time, was
founded on the raising again of the human soul
emerging alive from the body of dead matter.
The Corpus could not, and never did, come back,
or make its appearance again in any form, but
the spirit that arose from this was seen by Seers.

Religion proper commences with, and must
include, the idea or desire for another life.   This
belief in another life is founded on the resurrection of the Spirit.   The belief in the resurrection
of the Spirit was founded upon the faculties
of abnormal Seership.

So we have that beautiful ceremony in the M.M.
degree symbolical of this part of the Egyptian

Eschatology, as witnessed by the Ritual, and which the old Priests of Egypt worked in a much more beautiful and extended ceremony than we do. It was, in fact, the working of the M.M. and the 18° combined. It was the teaching, symbolically, of the life you should lead in this world and all you have to pass through in the next to obtain that promised life eternal.

These were all acted symbolically and dramatically, the more to impress it upon the Brothers, and the Signs and Symbols were brought on from the beginning. This was the secret Sign Language known to the Priests only. In some cases these have been changed as evolution progressed, but the decipherment of these ideographs proves that the interpretations are analogous ; and although we do not profess any religious doctrines in Freemasonry, *yet it is the highest form of religion conceivable in the human intellect.* You must please understand that " Amenta " was simply an " ideograph " to teach the Mysteries, and not believed to be a real passage through the Earth.

It is non-sectarian, and at the present day we have Brothers of all creeds meeting together in our Temples, without a particle of feeling of anything but that of Brotherhood. And why? Because Freemasonry was founded upon the religion of the ancient Egyptians, which was universal. Founded in the belief of the One Great Spirit, creator of all things. Founded on the rising again of the Spirit from the dead corpus. Founded on the tenets that are those of the Ritual of old Egypt.

At the downfall of the old Egyptian Empire the Priests of old Egypt were scattered over the face of the earth and water, some retaining one part of the Ritual, some another part ; and so many look upon them as various and different creeds, yet if you study these and find the origin of all, you will only arrive in the end at one source —old Egypt. That names and some forms and ceremonies have changed matters nothing ; it does not alter the original. That is the reason that we have Brothers of all creeds and denominations meeting together in one insoluble bond, and, in my opinion, it is one of the immutable laws of the Divine Creator that we shall, in some not far distant time, be all united again under one banner as of old. Whatever that name may be is immaterial, but it will be " Freemasonry," which possesses the truer form of the old Ritual than any other Cult.

THE GAVEL.

This Symbol (Fig. 24) was the original sacred sign used amongst primitive man (see Fig. 25), the Pygmies, the original homo, who were developed in Africa from an Anthropoid Ape. I have been amongst these little people, and with them it means " The Great One," " The Chief." It is just three sticks crossed, as you see. Now, let us trace the development of this to our present day, not as a theory, but as a fact—for the evidence and proofs are still extant. In following the evolution and history of the human race I find that two developments have been evolved out of this original sign, yet the meaning of the symbolism is the same in each.

First, amongst some of the Nilotic Negroes who

FIG. 24.   FIG. 25.   FIG.26.

followed the Pygmy all over the world and were a higher-developed type of man. (See " Origin and Evolution of Primitive Man.") They converted Fig. 25 into a double cross, Fig. 26, by placing the two sticks in a different way, and it is used amongst these people as one of their most sacred signs in their Totemic Ceremonies, and has been adopted by those who followed down to our present Christian and other Cults as one of their sacred signs, and is used by Brothers of the higher degrees. The symbolism and meaning are identical all through. Amongst the Stellar Mythos people (those who first reckoned time and kept their record by observation of the precession of the seven Pole Stars) it was used in the primary form, and is an Egyptian ideograph for Amsu—i.e. it is the first name given to the risen Horus, or, as Christians would say, the risen Christ. In a later phase, in the form of a double-headed Hammer or Axe, it was a symbol of the Great One, the Great Prince.

When primitive man began to learn more it became of great import, and amongst some tribes a special hut was built for it. The Priest and Great Chief were the only people allowed to see it. This is still extant at the present time amongst the Nilotic Negroes in Africa. In the Stellar Mythos it was also a symbol representing Horus —The Great Chief of the Hammer was one of his names ; The Cleaver of the Way ; the God of the Double Power, or Double Equinox—and it was brought on in the Solar Cult in the same way, when they recorded time by the sun's revolution. The Great God Ptah was not only the G.A.O.T.U., but was also called The Great Chief of the Hammer. (See Ritual.)

The proofs of this are found in the old Temples of Egypt, in the Ritual of Ancient Egypt, in Central and South America, Asia, and, as Evans found, at Knossos, where in the centre of the Temple were discovered three cubes, one surmounting the other, with an ideograph sign on each (Fig. 4), representing figuratively the Great One of the North=Horus I. ; The Great One of the South=Sut, El Shaddai of the Hebrews (who was originally primary god when they first worked out their Astro-Mythology in the Southern Hemisphere) ; The Great One of the Central=Shu, the God of the Equinox. This has been brought on in our Brotherhood as the symbol used and represented as in the Egyptian. It is the symbol of the Master, the double-headed hammer, the gavel, in Egyptian, Neter, as representing The Great and Powerful One, The One Great Chief —in our case, the great all-powerful one of the Lodge, the W. Master ; therefore I am sure you will agree with me that this is one of our symbols that has been handed down from the remotest antiquity ; but the symbolism has not changed through all the evolutions of the human race from the first to the present day, and we have the other two gavels, representatives of this Treble Cube in the J.W. and S.W. in this Lodge, and these are the representatives of the three Grand Originals in the R.A.C.

Now let us turn to the *date of origin* and *form of our Lodge*. Our Temples or Lodges first originated at the time of Totemic Sociology, over six hundred thousand years ago. These were formed at first in the seventeenth Nome of Upper

Egypt, and the Temples were built first as a circle,
then in the form of a double square, and at first
were not covered in, as far as we know ; simply
surrounded by walls made of stone with a Watcher
and Herald, both armed with a knife, at the
entrance. The ancient Egyptians, when working
out their Astro-Mythology, first divided the Heavens
into North and South—depicted by the two
Columns J. and B., and sometimes by two circles

FIG. 27.

(Fig. 27), then as a Triangle, next as
a Square, and finally as a Circle ; and
as they portrayed Heaven in these
forms, so in each case was the earth
symbolized—it was always a double
earth—i.e. the Earth and the Earth of
Eternity. The first things they noticed
at the Equinox were the Pole Stars,
those stars which never set.

Primitive man was evolved somewhere around
the Great Lakes, the source of the Nile in Africa,
and as he advanced in knowledge and worked out
his Astro-Mythology, he never forgot the tradition
of his home, which must have been handed down
verbally from generation to generation. It was
looked upon as the highest land or summit of the
earth, which they called Ta-Nuter, or Holy Land
—the Land of Spirits, or Khui Land, because it
was from here that the two Pole Stars, which
never set, could be seen resting on the horizon.

This was the summit of the Earthly Mount. The Two Eyes, side by side, was one mode of expressing this ideographically. The Pole Star, or The Eye, therefore, became a type of the Eternal, because, apparently, it never changed with time. It was the earliest ideographic type of supreme intelligence which gave the law in heaven, which was all-seeing, unerring, just, and true. It was the centre of the Circumpolar Paradise, and it became a standpoint in the heavens for the mind of man

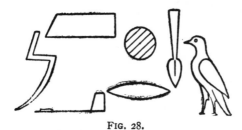

FIG. 28.

to rest on at the centre, and radiate to the circumference : *that point within a circle from which you could not err. But it was not here that you could find the secrets of a M.M. That is where we have gone wrong and made a bad innovation in our Ritual by not understanding the true gnosis. One must know all the secrets of a M.M. before arriving here, and it was in Amenta they learnt these, not in the Celestial Paradise at the North.* That is where the G.A.O.T.U. will receive you after you have travelled through the difficulties,

dangers, and valley of death, when the Soul has
been weighed by Ap-Senui and you are found
worthy to receive the password of the door leading
to eternal life (Fig. 28).

These were then represented by two poles, North
and South (the origin of our Columns J. and B.).
From these two Eyes there was therefore a
straight line from North Star to South (Fig. 29),
which was divided into two equal divisions by

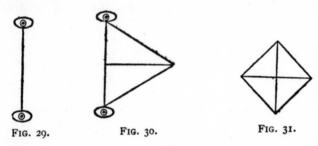

FIG. 29.   FIG. 30.   FIG. 31.

Shu at the Equinox, as in Fig. 30, Shu thus giving
the two Triangles of Sut and Horus, and then
the four quarters, or Square, was filled in and
formed later (Fig 31).

Heaven being now divided into four quarters, or
a Square, and the Earth being the same, it became
a double square, and all Temples throughout all
the world were built in this form as a representation of the Symbolisms of Earth and Heaven,
with the Pedestal of the Primary Trinity in the
Centre (Fig. 32). This was the universal plan
all through the Stellar and Lunar Mythos.

When the Solar Cult took the place of the Stellar and Lunar, Ptah, the G.A.O.T.U., figuratively worked out a tunnel through the Earth, called Amenta ; a passage for the Sun and Moon and Manes to go through the underworld, where all the difficulties, dangers, and trials had to be passed before entering that Circumpolar Paradise situated at the North. Before (i.e. during) the early part of the Stellar Cult the Manes passed through the underworld down beneath the earth—" The Great Void." During the Stellar Mythos Egypt was

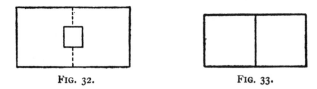

FIG. 32.   FIG. 33.

figuratively divided into a Square. The Manes entered at the North and passed South through this underworld, and came out in a cave situated on an Island in a Lake (The Great Lake, Victoria Nyanza and Tanganiki, which were then one—i.e. the Khui Land), the original place from whence the first man came, as well as the source of their water of life—the Nile—which they knew. This was worked out in the Stellar Mythos first.

The form of Amenta was given as a double square (Fig. 33) end to end—the double earth. Then Egypt was divided into two squares, the

North and South, and so you have the Crown of the North and the Crown of the South. In all Temples you find these were built in this form, the original being the House of Earth as a square, and the House of Eternity as a square, in the Stellar Mythos, surmounted by a Triangle. This again was represented in the formation of Amenta as a double square, the result being that as all Temples were built on this plan it did not change its form when the Cults changed ; for in the seven Lesser Mysteries and the ten Greater Mysteries you have this form of all Temples, and your Lodge is on the same plan, *but the orientation was changed*.

It is the origin of the form of our Lodge ; it is the origin of the form of all Temples, through all time, only during the Stellar Mythos the orientation for the first fifty-two thousand years was South, then for three hundred thousand years at least it was North, and after that in the Solar Cult and up to the present day it has been East. We do not have the Cubes in our Lodges, although the R.A.C. does, and this is the correct form. But in IRISH LODGES A CUBE IS IN THE CENTRE OF THE LODGE as an Altar, on which is placed the Warrant, Book of Constitutions, Working Tools, etc., and around it are stationed the three "Lesser Lights," which represent the Egyptian Primary Trinity. Thus the Irish Lodges retain

the true form, and, moreover, the Irish I. has
an address given to him pointing out what Freemasonry is, etc., just as the old priests of Egypt
gave their I. I use the term square and double
square because I do not like the American term,
nor do I think it correct. I prefer to use the term
" square " as the old Egyptians did, as this was
the primary, and in my opinion I don't think we
can improve upon their ideas. Although Amenta
might by some be termed " a cube," it was not
the idea of the Egyptians. This
is proved by the representative
ideographs of the Upper and Lower
Earth in the Ritual, viz. two ideographs for two skies (one reversed)
i.e. a sky for each (Fig. 34), which
proves that it was the same square
as in the former Cult.

FIG. 34.

Freemasonry is an Eschatology, taught originally in Signs and Symbols, these originating in
the mind of man from objective forms, and being
subjective representations of sublime tenets which
at this early period he had no words to express
otherwise, and which afterwards became the secret
and sacred writings and language of the Priests.
Signs preceded words and words preceded writings.
These teach you the highest ideals and conceptions that the human intellect has ever evolved,
both morally and eschatologically, and how you

11

should live in this world to gain that everlasting
life and happiness promised to us in that spiritual
form which all must assume at no great distance
of time.

We are all striving to obtain a knowledge of
" a something " which we feel there is, there must
be, but many cannot yet understand what it is, and
how to obtain it. There is that written on stone
and on papyri (which has been preserved through
hundreds of thousands of years) showing what we
should do in this world to gain that everlasting
life and happiness in the next, given by the Divine
Creator to our forefathers, and the tenets of which,
to a great extent, have been preserved to us
Freemasons direct from the original.

VIII

FREEMASONRY, PAST AND FUTURE

A Lecture delivered before the Mid Kent Masters' Lodge, No. 3173, at Chatham, on the 15th March, 1913.

THERE are very few students amongst our Brotherhood ; and even amongst those few scarcely one who can go beyond the "Modern Aspect" of Freemasonry ; I have chosen, therefore, to discuss the "Ancient Origin" of Freemasonry, not the Modern Aspect, which covers a period of a few hundreds of years only. Bros. Gould, Anderson, Armitage, Horsley, Lawrence, and many other able writers and speakers have studied the latter. We have no written history of the Craft prior to that time, only traditions. Yet Freemasonry has existed for at least six hundred thousand years, but not under the name of Freemasonry. That term did not then exist. The farthest date back in which we find that word is 1376. But the word or term "Craftsman" was in existence more than six hundred thousand years ago, as were some of our Signs, Symbols,

and Rituals.   Freemasonry was then the religion
of the world ; it existed not in this country only,
but throughout Africa, Europe, Asia, America, and
many islands in the Pacific.

You may ask, How do I know this? It is
because I have been enabled to read the writings
on the wall still existing in the old ruined cities,
and on various papyri that have been found in
different parts of the world.   Moreover, I discovered that these people were all of one Cult or
Brotherhood, analogous in every particular to our
own Brotherhood, and my knowledge of geology
has assisted me in arriving at these conclusions as
regards the vast ages of time.   It is only by going
back to the primary and tracing the human race
from the beginning, the signs and symbols then
formed as sign language in substitution for the
articulate sounds, which at that time did not
exist such as we have now, and following the
history of the " rise and fall " of all great nations,
and the causes for the same, that the secrets of
the past can be unravelled.

Having done this, after critically examining all
existing evidence, one conclusion only can be
arrived at, and it is that our Brotherhood
originated with the old Mystery Teachers, or High
Priests, in Old Egypt, whence various exodes
spread throughout the world, carrying with them
all the Rituals, Signs, and Symbols of the Brother-

hood, primarily as Stellar Cult, and at a later date the Solar Eschatology. That this was so is proved by what we still find extant in many countries, i.e. all our Signs and Symbols, with engraved hieroglyphics explaining them by their side as an objective proof, and their hieroglyphic writings on papyri as subjective evidence.

It must have taken hundreds of thousands of years to spread throughout the world, in view of the fact that presumedly journeys had to be made on foot at this early period of the world's existence.

The lowest strata of the earth's surface where remains of Stellar Cult man have been found is in the Pliocene Age, in Italy, which must date back six hundred thousand years or more. Also the Piltdown skull of a human found in Sussex.[1] Hence the proof of the great antiquity of man's existence on this earth as against the Biblical date, and however much some Brothers may express their disbelief of the ages of time I have mentioned, they cannot gainsay or go against this geological fact ; it is sufficient proof.

I want you to go back with me for a few minutes, so far away in the past, to the time when man had not the articulate language that we have now, and so expressed some of his ideas and thoughts in

[1] This is debatable—if this Piltdown skull was in the Pliocene or not.

Signs and Symbols.   Many conclusions arrived at
were founded on the observation of the elemental
powers and observation of natural phenomena.   If
you will bear this in mind, you will be able to
understand better the reason for the origin of our
Signs and Symbols, and why these have continued
to be associated and represented in every religious
cult with very little or no alteration from the
original.   Many of our Signs and Symbols were
brought on prior to the Stellar Cult ; but it was
during this period that the Great Pyramids, as
well as the Temples, were built, which are found
nearly all over the world.   The old Brotherhood
was one and the same in forms, rites, and ceremonies, with the same Signs and Symbols in Africa,
Asia, Europe, America, and some of the Pacific
isles.

The Stellar Cult people's Temples and buildings
can always be identified, because they were iconographic, whereas the Solar people's were not ; they
both built with polygonal-shaped stones and
monoliths.   Therefore you can always distinguish
definitely the ages of these Temples and who built
them, and the reason was that in the Stellar Cult
pre-human types were used, i.e. Zootypes, to
represent the Great Architect of the Universe and
His attributes ; whereas in the Solar the human
types had taken the place of these.   Their Temples
were of the same form and shape as ours, except

that they had the Pedestal, which the R.A.M.'s have, and which in the old Temples was always situated in the centre. These two different degrees, as we have made them, were then only one, as can be seen at the Temples of Knossos and those in Central America.

The door of the Temple was an equilateral triangle, and therefore a Symbol of Heaven (Fig. 35). The Square was a Symbol of Earth ; the whole entrance symbolized passing of the Soul from earth to heaven.

The two Pillars at the porchway entrance of every Temple are specially important in ancient symbolism. Originally these old Mystery Teachers divided the heavens into two divisions, North and South, which was represented by the Pole, or Pillar of Set, in the South—El Shaddai of the Phœnicians ; and the Pole, or Pillar of Horus, in the North, termed the " Sustainers of the Heavens." Sometimes two Eyes were portrayed as the two Poles, or, rather, two Pole Stars. These were the representative symbols of the two gods of the Pole Stars, North and South, called also the Two Judges. The Ideographs of them were Two Jackals, and were later called in Egyptian the two Tatt Pillars, one meaning " In Strength " and the other " To establish "; and combined Tattu, which in Egyptian also means " The place of estab-

FIG. 35.

lishing for ever." The four lines at the top represent the Celestial and Terrestrial Worlds.

The next division was symbolized by the division of heaven in two circles, North and South. (These we find in many places in Cornwall and Scotland, and throughout the world.) This was the first and oldest form of the Temple in the world, a circle of twelve stones. After this, the next phase of heaven was depicted by two Triangles; No. 1, Fig. 36, was the Ideographic name and symbol for Set, and

No. 2, Fig. 36, was the Ideographic name and symbol of Horus. At a later epoch these two Triangles were joined (see Fig. 8) as a representative symbol for heaven, or the Land of the Spirits or Gods; and when Horus became Primary

FIG. 36.

God of the North and superseded Set, the Primary God of the South, these were afterwards depicted as Fig. 7, and this was associated with the name of Horus only. It represents, in the Egyptian, " Ra Harmachus "; another name was Aiu, the God of the Double Horizon, which was one of the forms of Horus; it was from this part of the old Egyptian Eschatology that the Hebrew Cult was founded.

These two triangles must be of great interest to you because of the various forms in which they are portrayed—curiously enough, on your own notice sent out I find one form, Fig. 37, which is prac-

tically the same as Fig. 7, with the all-seeing eye
in the centre. These triangles, in another phase,
form the five-pointed star (Fig. 38). In this
latter there should be a point in the centre, which
we have left out, but in the original it was there ;

FIG. 37.

FIG. 38.

it was the point in the centre of a circle (Fig. 39),
equal to the point at the top of the triangle
or cone (Fig. 40), that was crowned with the star
at the summit and has the same meaning as the

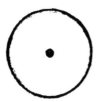

FIG. 39.

FIG. 40.

Eye. The Eye is an Ideograph of the Pole
Star, and two eyes therefore symbols of the
two Pole Stars, but at the time that the two
triangles were blended in the form of Fig. 7
the Eye was an Ideograph of the Pole Star North,

associated with Horus only. This one, the centre
of the six other Pole Stars of Ursa Minor, or
Little Bear, revolved in a circle around this centre
one, therefore the Pole Star was a symbol or
type of the eternal, because apparently it never
changed with time. It was the earliest type of
supreme intelligence which gave the law, which
was unerring, just, and true, and it became a
standpoint in the heavens for the mind of man
to rest on at the centre and radiated to the circumference (a point within a circle from which one
could not err). It was also a type or symbol of
the Judge, or Just One. This will give you the
origin and meaning of the symbols you use on
your stationery, which are associated with these
two triangles. The interpretation is that this is the
symbol of the Just God who gave the Law ; The
Great Architect of the Universe. As regards " That
point within a circle," a bad innovation has been
made here, on account of not knowing the true
gnosis of the Ritual of Ancient Egypt, as this
was not the place that all the secrets were communicated and known ; " This Centre of the
Circle " represented Paradise. They left the East
to go to the West to obtain the secrets of M.M.
These secrets were given in " Amenta," which was
entered in the West, and traversed until they came
out in the East, before they could enter Paradise
situated at the North. The secrets were taught and

given in Amenta, which was portrayed as an Ideographic Symbol, to teach the Mysteries, and was not believed to be anything but Mythical by the old wise men of Egypt ; the old Mystery Teachers. The D.C. of the 18° corresponds to Amenta in our teachings.

The next evolution was the heavens in the form of a Square, and as they portrayed a uranographic picture here so they depicted the earth—thus you have two Squares, the later form of the two Triangles, and it was in this form they built the Temples, a double square end to end, with the cubes in the centre to mark the division between Heaven and Earth. On the top of the cube was a circle of gold enclosing the Sacred Triangle, and at each corner was the Ideographic name of one of the Primary Trinity, or the Three Grand Originals (Fig. 41).

FIG. 41.

Thus you see the progressive evolution of the mind of man as depicted by the different Signs and Symbols he used to express his thoughts and beliefs when he had no language as we have now.

1. He divided the Heavens into North and South, and symbolized this by the Two Pillars— that of Set for the South and that of Horus for the North.

2. The two Pole Stars, N. and S., were de-

picted as two Eyes, also as symbols of Set and Horus as the Two Judges.

3. Then we have the Heavens divided into two Circles, the North for Horus and the South for Set.

4. The next is the Heavens symbolized by the two Triangles into the two equal divisions, with the same meaning as the Circles.

5. In the next portrayal, Set, or the South Pole Star, has sunk down below the horizon as the old people came North from the Equatorial Provinces of Africa, where they were born or originated, and the Pole Star North has risen in the Heavens, i.e. Horus has become the highest and supreme one and appropriated all the attributes of Set unto himself ; and now—

6. The Heavens are represented as a Square. The two Triangles merged into one, which has four supports, symbolized as the brothers or children of Horus.

7. The Pole Star North (Horus) represented by one Eye now becomes " The All-Seeing Eye," a type of the Great Judge of All (Fig. 14).

These Symbols and Signs were used by these old Mystery Teachers to represent the Great Architect of the Universe and His various attributes when they had no language of words to express their thoughts as we have now. This was part of their Sign Language—their sacred symbols which have been handed on from generation to generation to the present day, the interpretation varying somewhat with each successive Cult.

So many, even learned men, who ought to know better, have stated verbally and in writing that the old Egyptians worshipped many gods, birds, cats, and other animals, etc. This was not so. These old Priests, the forefathers of our Brotherhood, only believed and worshipped One Great God, the Great Architect of the Universe, expressed by various Signs and Symbols. If the Triangle was the sign and symbol of the Great God, it was the Great God that was worshipped, and not the Triangle. The Triangle was held sacred because it was a symbol made to represent Him. In twenty thousand years' time it is quite possible that those who come after us and find " the Lamb " sculptured in our churches will say that we were worshippers of sheep—which would be just as true as many say of the old Egyptians at the present time. If the Symbol represented the Deity, it was the Deity that was worshipped and not the Symbol.

Bro. Hobbs, in a letter to *The Freemason*, states that I speak derisively of Thomas Payne and others who attribute the origin of the Craft as Druidical. Let me state here distinctly I did nothing of the kind. What I said was that Payne and others stated that these old Druids worshipped the Sun,

Moon, and Stars, but I say it was not so. These were symbols either representing the Deity or some of His attributes, which the Druids perfectly understood, but which the learned men of the present day do not, and have taken the shadow for the substance and mixed them up, which will not help to understand the Wisdom of Ancient Egypt, or give any knowledge or meaning of all you find of the peoples of past ages.

Many would wish to know how these have been handed on from the time they came into existence up to the time you found them used in your Lodges. The answer to this, fully set forth, with the proofs, would fill a big volume ; I will, however, try and explain in a few words so that you will be able to think out the details as I have done.

To commence with, all the sacred Signs and Symbols first used by these old Mystery Teachers in their Stellar Cult were brought on into their Lunar and Solar Cults, and from the Solar Eschatology, the earliest Christians, the Copts, adopted them. Some of the original forms have been slightly changed, others were discarded by the later Christians ; examples of this you can find in many old churches here in England ; one in particular, Launceston Church, in Cornwall, is rich in the early emblems which were worked here in stone and built in by the old Druidical Priests, who became Christians between 1000 and 1500. In Mr. Harold Bayley's books you will find numerous examples. They are also to be found in the churches of the Abyssinians. That the Chinese have them is because these are old Stellar Cult people, who left Egypt at the time that the hieroglyphic language was undergoing the evolution of having affixes and prefixes added to the original Ideograph, and before the Hieratic and Demotic were evolved. That the Hindoos and Jews have them is because these were Solar Mythos people when they left Egypt, and are still so (in two different forms or epochs of time), so that many are thinking at the present day that all these people have different religions, yet in reality it is not so. Names have changed, language has become reflected instead of monosyllabic, therefore the majority now express in words, in different ways, what was formerly sign language ; the origin of all was one and the same, and because some have travelled by one road and some by another, and have different tales to tell of the routes by which they travelled, you must not lose sight and meaning of the originals. You can trace them all back the way they came, as you can trace them all from the earliest to the present time—if you will only leave out the dogmas that have been introduced.

The old Brothers were the men of the highest

learning and integrity in all countries, and had to
be proven before they could be admitted at each
higher grade they attained to.   None of the
common and unlearned were ever admitted to their
secrets or Brotherhood, and this is the reason why
we do not admit slaves into our Brotherhood.

What was the cause of the destruction and
supposed loss of all their old Eschatology, or
Doctrine of Final Things?

When Egypt was at its zenith dissensions arose
amongst the Priests, and, as the inevitable result,
Socialism followed.   No peoples have ever risen
to be a great nation and then fallen and been
destroyed except for these two primary causes,
and no downfall was so great as that of Egypt.

Their Temples were thrown down and given over
to fire and sword, and their old writings were
burned, or lost, or became unintelligible to the
destroyer.   But we find that remnants of the old
Priesthood who were our old Brothers escaped ;
others had been established in other countries, as,
for example, the Druids in this country and in
the North of France and in America ; these again
had to flee before the sword.

The old faith was never entirely lost, however,
but was kept secret and sacred by a scattered few,
and you must remember that their Signs, Symbols,
and the meaning of their Rituals were only known
to a chosen few—men of unimpeachable character,

integrity, and honour, who have been tried and tested. From these few, we, the present Brotherhood of Freemasons, have been evolved ; we have risen out of the ashes of past ages to form a Brotherhood throughout the world again, as of old, with all the same Signs, Symbols, sacred rites and ceremonies.

Many innovations have become necessary to replace some of the lost secrets, and to meet the higher state of evolution which humanity has now attained. For instance, for the true password for M.M.—Maat-Heru in Egyptian, meaning one whose voice must be obeyed—we have substituted another ; also in our passwords for grips we have substituted our present for the original—in fact, there are several in the various degrees, but I know all in the Egyptian from the first to the thirty-third, and I do not think it matters now to attempt any change. During the last hundred years the Brotherhood has been striving to raise itself again towards " the greater standard " and to attain a higher evolution.

This is a short résumé of the Past, and there is no time at my disposal to bring forward all proofs of that which I have stated ; indeed, all the proofs that I have found would occupy many large volumes, but in my " Signs and Symbols of Primordial Man," Second Edition, there are more proofs given. It is a book that took me twenty years to complete, but it was a labour of love, because it was written for the information of the Brotherhood " who could not read the writings on the wall." But it is not a work which is perfect by any means. It is written to guide and interest you in the right road to the knowledge you wish to obtain ; a small path cut through a dense, dark forest, which I hope others will broaden and enlarge.

Much has been said lately on the subject of Freemasonry and religion. Many Brethren, and some of them very eminent and learned divines, have stated—and no doubt they would not make the statement if they did not believe it—" that Freemasonry is not a religion." Brothers, my contention is that Freemasonry is the greatest, truest, and purest religion in the world, for these reasons :

1. Religion proper commences with and must include the idea or desire for and belief in another life.

2. This belief in another life is founded on the belief of the resurrection of the Spirit.

3. We all believe in one great God, the Great Architect of the Universe.

4. Therefore we all believe in the rising again of the human soul, emerging alive from the body of dead matter. This body of dead matter could not come back or rise again, if disintegrated, but the Spirit could.

5. In our teachings, in our forms and ceremonies which are dramatically performed, we are taught how we should live in this world, and how we should die, to attain that great end of everlasting happiness which is the one object all the Brotherhood profess and desire to attain._ Therefore this is the greatest, truest, and purest religion in the world, void of all dogmas, one in which poor humanity can work together in perfect harmony, and one in which there cannot be any dissensions to disturb the fraternal feelings which should always exist between us, and may it ever continue to be the same.

We have no history for those who cannot read ancient writings except a decipherment and translation of some of these symbols and workings which I have given, which probably many have never heard of, few have read, and which are ignored by some or adversely criticized by others, who are not acquainted with the knowledge of these decipherments, and who cannot read the writings on the walls. Few Brothers have studied the history and evolution of the human race, and the religious conceptions during the evolution, which alone contain the secret of the development of Freemasonry. Without a knowledge of the past there can be no guide to the future.

And what of the future? It is only by studying the past that you can gain a true knowledge of what Freemasonry is. At present many are only in the analogous position of the poor aboriginal natives of Australia and other countries. You have forms, ceremonies, Signs, Symbols, and Ritual, which you repeat, and act, without understanding their true origin and meaning—as they do in their Totemic ceremonies—but that is not what true Freemasonry is ; nor is being letter perfect, or a good orator, or a dramatist. These points are to be highly appreciated ; they enhance the greater solemnity of our ceremonies, and photograph our beautiful Ritual more indelibly on the mind of the initiate ; but if we do not act those principles in our lives outside the Lodge, which we so solemnly promise in the Lodge, what frauds we are !

The past and continuous thought of the majority of our Brotherhood is one of self, rightly when it especially affects themselves—Feasting and Charities. But within the last few years a very bright star has arisen in Freemasonry. There are many in the Craft who are striving to bring about that high ideal of Brotherhood to be a reality, and not a sham, although they have little encouragement from the powers that govern the Order.

I congratulate you Brothers of the Mid-Kent Masters' Lodge on being amongst those that are striving to elevate our Brotherhood, because the meeting together, the reading of lectures on the many subjects that are of vital importance to the Craft, the discussions that follow on these, cannot but result in a vast amount of good. Whether the papers are considered good, bad, or indifferent, the results obtained in the end must be to the advantage of the Brethren.

Although we are the greatest Charity in the world, and that is the only thing that interests many—which, so far, is right and good—yet that is not Freemasonry, nor will Freemasonry ever be advanced farther in evolution, or coalescing the Brotherhood into one great fraternal and universal whole by it. The One Great Universal Brotherhood, each individual carrying out those sublime tenets he was taught in the Lodge in his daily life outside the Lodge, is what Freemasonry should and must attain. Many Brothers do not think, and therefore do not practise these things outside the Lodge.

It is the action of the individual Mason in discharging with great fidelity every duty he has in this life, both outside the Lodge as well as within, that will raise the Fraternity. How can we hope to attain Universal Brotherhood without setting the example in this the mother country to our present Brotherhood throughout the world? If the mother is careless and indifferent, her children will become careless and indifferent. The whole Brotherhood of the world look up to you for example and precept. How jealous, therefore, should you be to exemplify to the world that every Mason should carry out the tenets in action, and not in platitude only.

Then let there be no discord and divisions amongst you, because, if these predominate, instead of establishing the unity of Universal Brotherhood, the human brotherhood becomes more and more widely separated. Let there exist a perfect unity of sentiment between you ; or, if there must be a difference, let it be of emulation in the exercise of those good qualities which, while they dignify our nature, add lustre to the highest and beauty to the lowest station. Let the principles and precepts of morality and fervent piety, which are continually ascending from our altars, repress every unkind thought and smooth every asperity of feeling.

And why should this not be so?

The answer remains with yourselves, and in the action of your daily lives. You can all attain the ideal if you try, and if all strive then the Brotherhood will be a living reality, with the power of governing the world for human happiness. I believe it is only a question of time before our great ideal will be realized. Freemasonry during the last fifty years has made much progress, and even within the last few years has raised itself towards that standard, and the number of Brothers who are working to attain that goal has so increased every year, that the outlook for the future of Freemasonry is very bright. But we want more workers and we want a higher standard generally. We have no dogmas or creeds to confuse the faith and belief in the One Great Eternal and Divine Architect of the Universe, Creator of all things. Therefore no question of a difference of creed could obtrude itself or cause any secessions amongst the Brothers of various climes and countries. By your universal combination you possess the dominant power for the advancement, for the good of humanity generally.

For Freemasonry to exist there is no way of standing still. It must progress or it must fall. This must be the question for you to answer : Is it to be Past, or Future?

Therefore let each one steadily follow that Bright Star which has arisen. It is striving to throw its rays of light amongst us, and bring about that great ideal of Universal Brotherhood, so as to make the future of Freemasonry a great reality, and not an ideal in name only.

IX

THE ORIGIN AND EXPLANATION OF SOME MASONIC SIGNS AND SYMBOLS

A Lecture delivered before the Hendre Lodge, No. 3250, at the Masonic Temple, Cardiff, 24th April, 1913.

WALES, in conjunction with the West of England, Devon and Cornwall, is particularly rich in possessing remains of old Temples and stones, on which many Signs and Symbols are still extant, and can be seen ; hence you will recognize that here you possess objective proofs, and are therefore able the better to appreciate and follow me than many other Brothers who are not so rich in the possession of Sacred Symbols. I always feel a pleasure in giving information upon the origin and meaning of all our Signs and Symbols and Rituals, as without a knowledge of the Astro-Mythology and Eschatology of old Egypt it is impossible to decipher and find the true interpretation of these Signs and Symbols.

To understand the meaning and origin of these we have to go back and return again by the road we came, far away back, six hundred thousand

years ago. The remains of skeletons found in
the Pliocene strata were of the present type of man,
and were Stellar Mythos people, as was proved by
the implements found with them. This is sufficient
evidence alone, because these must date at least
six hundred thousand years ago, probably much
more.

There is at the present time a learned American
Professor excavating the Temples of the Sphinx,
who, like many others, understands nothing about
the old Cults of Egypt, and is writing the greatest
nonsense about this figure. One statement in
particular I would draw your especial attention
to. He states that "the Sphinx is much older than
the Pyramids," which is quite wrong. The Great
Pyramid was built by the Stellar Cult people, and
has portrayed in its figure all their astronomical
knowledge, and their cults, in Sign language. The
Sphinx was built by the early Solar people,
thousands of years after, and represents Ra Harmachus, God of the Double Horizon. The proof
of this is that the Sphinx itself has spoken once,
and you will find this on the stele of Tahtmes IV,
where it is called the Sphinx of Khepra, who
was a form of Harmachus, of whom I shall have
to say more later on ; but the whole of the early
Solar Cult is portrayed in this figure in Sign language, and may be easily deciphered and translated by those who understand. But when

professors write their theories, not understanding Sign language, or the old Cults of Ancient Egypt, it does an immense harm, because, coming from the pen of a professor, people generally take it that it must be true, whereas it is puerile nonsense. Modern ignorance of the mythical mode of representation has led to the ascribing of innumerable false beliefs.

These Stellar Cult people were the first to build Temples. They built the Great Pyramid and many of the old Temples found in Africa, Europe, Asia, America, and some of the islands of the Pacific. Their Priests, who were their learned men, were the old Mystery Teachers of Egypt ; many exodes of them left Egypt and carried all their knowledge of building and their religion to most parts of the world. These were followed by a higher class and developed human—namely, the Solar Cult people.

The buildings of the Stellar people can always be identified by their being Iconographic, whereas the Solar and others were not. Therefore, you can always distinguish definitely the ages of the Temples, and who built them. These people were the first to work out the old Astro-Mythology, and it is to this that we owe the origin of many of our Sacred Signs and Symbols. It is important to distinguish and know the difference, because the Stellar is so much older, and yet the Solar is only a further evolution of the Stellar.

These old Mystery Teachers first divided the Heavens into two parts, the North and the South, which they symbolized by two Poles or Pillars, one belonging to the North, and one to the South (see Fig. 15). These were called the two sustainers of Heaven ; also they represented the two Gods of the Pole Stars, and later, in Egyptian, were named the two Tatt Pillars. These two Pillars were always placed at the porchway entrance of every Temple in the world, and represent J. and B. in our Masonic Temples.

The next portrayal of Heaven was symbolized by two circles representing a Pre-Zodiacal formation of the Heavens in the Stellar Mythos. Fig. 27 represents the North (Horus) and the South (Set) respectively, which in Temple building were formed of twelve monoliths. Remains of these Circles, with twelve stones to each, may be seen in Wales, Cornwall, Scotland, India, America, and many other parts of the world. These represent the very first form of Temples built by man, and preceded the Temples in the form of a double square by many thousands of years. Probably these were not covered in. Much more could be said regarding these, but they are just mentioned to show their origin and meaning.

In the next phase of representation we find Heaven depicted by two Triangles. These two Triangles are specially important in ancient symbolism, more especially on account of the various portrayals of combinations we find. In Wales and the West of England many are to be found, as well as in all countries where the old Stellar and Solar people traversed. The first phase of the two Triangles was as 1, Fig. 6, which is an Ideograph for the name of Set—El Shaddai of the Phœnicians—and represented the God of the Pole Star South, as well as the southern division of Heaven ; and 2, which is an Ideographic symbol for Horus, represents the God of the Pole Star North and the northern division of Heaven. At a later epoch these two Triangles were joined (see Fig. 8) as a representative symbol for Heaven or the land of the Spirits. Sometimes we find these doubled, as in Fig. 21, where the two Double Triangles are surrounded by four Serpents, representing symbolically the four Powers which guard the Land of the Spirits, as in Revelation " guarded the Throne and around about the Throne," called in Egyptian the Khui Land. A still later portrayal was a treble form of these, surrounded by concentric circles, as in Fig. 22.

The meaning of all three forms is the same wherever found throughout the world, but one form is more ancient than the other. They are given here as they occurred in evolution. This Ideograph for the Khui Land, or the Land of the Spirits, was the most Sacred Symbol amongst our ancient

Brothers, and still is so amongst the remnants of the Stellar Cult people living at the present time. The reason why we have two Triangles combined or blended into one symbol, or figure, as on our own Masonic jewels, calls for some explanation.

Primordial man was born in Africa ; you will find proofs of this in my book " Origin and Evolution of Primitive Man." About the region of the head of the Nile Valley, or Great Lakes, man could see and mark the two Pole Stars—North and South. The South was associated with Set, and the North with Horus. Then Set was primary God ; his Triangle or Ideograph was as 1 in Fig. 6. As these people left their old land and travelled to the North, the South Pole Star would sink down below the Horizon, and the North Pole Star would rise in the Heavens and become the only one visible, which was represented by the Ideograph for Horus (2 in Fig. 6). This is the mythical representation of Shu lifting up the Heavens. Horus was then given all the attributes of Set, and the triangle of Set became blended with the triangle of Horus, and formed these double triangles in various phases, which were associated with the name of Horus only, first in the Stellar Cult and later carried on in their Solar Cult, and some of them afterwards into the Christian doctrines. One combination formed of these two triangles is that

with the All-seeing Eye in the centre (Fig. 42).
This form is an Ideographic symbol for Horus, as
God of the Pole Star North and South, having the
" All-seeing Eye." This originated with these old
Stellar Cult people. At the Equatorial Provinces
the two Pole Stars could be seen resting on the
Horizon, and these were symbolized in one form,
as two Eyes, called Merti in Egyptian (Fig. 13).
In Egyptian these two Eyes were, therefore, Ideo-
graphs for the two Pole Stars ; but when the South
Pole Star had disappeared below the Horizon, and

FIG. 42.

FIG. 43.

the North Pole Star had risen in the Heavens, there
was only one Eye (Fig. 14). The North Pole
Star had figuratively absorbed the South, and this
North Pole Star became a symbol or type of the
Eternal, because apparently it never changed with
time. It was the earliest type of supreme intelli-
gence which gave the law which was unerring,
just, and true. It was also a type or symbol of the
Great Judge, or Just One. The interpretation,
therefore, of this symbol, sign, or ideograph
(Fig. 42) is Horus, or T.G.A.O.T.U., the
Eternal Lord of the North and South, the Great

Judge, Unerring, Just, and True, Lord of the All-seeing Eye. This was always associated with Horus of the Stellar Cult only.

There is still another form of the Triangle, or rather a combination of the two, as in Fig. 43, which represents a Star with five points, a more ancient formation than the previous one, which, in its true form, belonged to the Stellar Cult people only. Many may not at first recognize that this is a combination of the same two Triangles, but if you will follow the mode of formation, as in

FIG. 44.

FIG. 45.

Figs. 44 and 45, it will be seen that it is so. The upper part of Set's Triangle (44 AAA) is cut off and attached to or joined to the Triangle of Horus. Also see that the base line or divisional line at the equinox (Fig. 45 B) has been removed or is absent, and there is a reason for this, which speaks for itself, in symbolic language. It portrays graphically that Set's Triangle was given to Horus when he became primary God of the Pole Star North. In the oldest formations of this symbol there was a dot or Star in the centre, which is equal to the Eye given in other representations.

The interpretation is the same in each case, i.e. these are Ideographic Signs or Symbols for Horus, God of the Pole Star North, and South, and his abode. I am giving this Symbol and Sign with interpretation and proofs fully, because in my lecture at Chatham, at the Mid-Kent Masters' Lodge, seeing it used on their stationery, I gave a short explanation of it, but there was one Brother who doubted my decipherment. And I see that it is also the jewel of the Hendre Lodge. I therefore thought it incumbent on myself to bring forward conclusive and critical proofs now. Although it is used as a Sacred Symbol by the Jews, it was brought on from the old Stellar Cult. The Jews left out the " All-seeing Eye," and, therefore, tried to convert it into a Symbol of Horus of the Double Horizon, or Ihuh, in their terminology, but the original had the dot or eye in the centre. It was never intended to be a Sign or Symbol of Horus of the Double Horizon originally. It was a Symbol of the abode of Horus, God of the North and South, God of the All-seeing Eye, and proof of this is the fact that it has the phonetic signification of sb aau —in Egyptian, " Abode of Stars," or " Subdivision of the Celestial World," which was situated at the North. You will find this in the list of Ideographs of Bunsen's Dictionary, p. 497. (Fig. 46.) That alone is a sufficient proof. It might be translated as " The Abode or House of Horus " in one phase

—i.e. Paradise. You have "Hendre" portrayed in its centre, so that must be your representation, terrestrially, of the Celestial—very appropriate.

Sometimes you will only find one Triangle with a dot or a star at the apex, as in Fig. 47. This also is an Ideograph for Horus, God of the Pole Star North. All the above forms belong to the Stellar Cult people and not to any other. In Fig. 48 the Triangle of Horus has been brought on into the Christian doctrines ; the Symbol here given has been taken from the Lapiderian Gallery

FIG. 46.

FIG. 47.

FIG. 48.

of the Vatican (Lundy, p. 92) and the Cross added in the centre with the Ru.

We will now trace how these Triangles were brought on from the Stellar and appropriated by the Solar people, when the latter Cult succeeded the former. The first combination of these two Triangles in the Solar is found in many countries, as in Fig. 49, sometimes surrounded by a circle, as in Fig. 50. This Double Triangle has been wrongly called "Solomon's Seal," but although still used as a Sacred Sign by the Hebrews, it

represents in Egyptian "Ra Harmachus," or Aiu
or Iu, the God of the Double Horizon, from which
their Cult originated. It was one of the names
of Horus, and was associated with the name of
Horus only in the Solar Cult, therefore it is more
than a hundred thousand years older than Solomon.

This form of the Double Triangle is one which
should always be differentiated from these other
two. Although the Symbol in each case is formed
by a crossing and overlapping of one Triangle
superimposed on the other, yet the interpretation is

FIG. 49.

FIG. 50.

different. In these two Triangles, Figs. 42 and
43, the interpreted meaning is the same, that these
are Symbols, or Ideographs, for Horus, or
T.G.A.O.T.U., God of the Pole Stars North and
South, and belong to the Stellar Cult only ;
whereas in the form of Fig. 49 it is an
early Solar Symbol, and an Ideograph of Horus,
God of the Double Horizon—Aiu, Iu, or Iau. It
goes to prove that progressive evolution took place
in the human brain thousands of years ago, and
how one cult was brought on from the preceding

one, the same Symbols being made use of in many cases.

Another very interesting proof that this Symbol belongs to the God of the Double Horizon, and

The Idol Tandayudhaswami.

FIG. 51.

that it is an early Solar Symbol and not Stellar, may be deduced from a very interesting paper read before the Dorset Masters' Lodge by Bro. Herbert Bradley, C.S.I., P.Dis.G.M. Madras, in

which he gives the photograph of what he calls
the Idol Tandayudhaswami (Dorset Masters'
Lodge Transactions, 1910-11), in which this
Double Triangle is depicted on the idol's back surrounded by a circle (Fig. 51). This, therefore,
is a Symbolic representation of " Atum "-Horus, in
the form of Atum-Iu—the first God of the Solar
Cult under several names in many countries. Bro.

Seal made by Caste Hindoos.

FIG. 52.   FIG. 53.

Bradley has also given an interesting photograph
of a Seal used by Caste Hindoos in making Caste
Marks (see Figs. 52 and 53), in which appears the
original Double Triangle with the eye in the centre,
symbolic of God of the Pole Star North and South.
Therefore, whatever cult these people profess now,
Hindoo or otherwise, they are direct descendants
of the old Stellar Cult people—this, their most
sacred sign, stamps them as such. (I wish to
express my sincere thanks to Bros. Herbert Bradley

and Sherren, P.G. Sec. Dorset, for permission to reproduce these illustrations.)

Another form, or combination, of the Triangle must be especially interesting to Welshmen, because you find it so often portrayed in Wales, and this was a Sacred Symbol amongst the Druids. It is found all over the world where the Solar Cult existed. It is the Triangle with the Swastika in the centre, Fig. 54, which is another Ideograph for Horus as God of the Four Quarters, or

FIG. 54.

FIG. 55.

FIG. 56.

God of the Double Horizon, and is frequently associated with the Symbols, Figs. 55 and 56, which have the phonetic value of Iu, or Iau. Three feathers, or rods, or rays of light ; this was also one of the most sacred signs amongst the Druids or Solar Cult people. It is another Ideograph for Horus under the name of Iu or Iau, or Ea or Aiu, God of the Double Horizon. There are various names throughout the world for this Symbol. It was also the symbol for the name of Egypt, as may be seen in Pierrot's Dictionary, page 754. (Fig. 57.)

It must be especially interesting to Welshmen because these feathers, or rods, or rays of light, represent the feathers adopted "as totemic badge" for the Prince of Wales. He not only wears these feathers as Prince of Wales, but because they are also the Sign and Symbol of " The Prince or King of Egypt," as they are the Ideographic Symbol for Egypt. Then, again, it is the Ideograph for Iu, or Iau, who was the son of the God Atum. So here we have a curious and interesting fact, namely, the Prince of Wales is

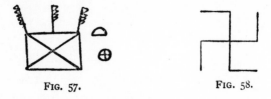

FIG. 57.   FIG. 58.

the Son of our Earthly King, so he represents in a terrestrial form Iu, the son of his father Atum, in a Celestial or Spiritual form, this sacred Sign or Symbol being common to each. This has never been explained or deciphered by any one but myself, and there are some interesting hypotheses associated with this, which I am unable to discuss in our Masonic Lodge, and I am quite sure His Royal Highness is not acquainted with these facts or the real origin of his "Three feathers."

I wish particularly to draw attention to the Symbol of the Swastika, Fig. 58, for three

reasons.   First because our old Brothers used it,
and the Operative Masons still have this Symbol
in their ceremonies ; next because this sign was
at a later period converted into the Cross which
our Brothers of the 18° use (see how this con-
version took place in " Signs and Symbols of
Primordial Man "), and because the interpretation given by the Operative Masons for this Sign
is not correct—in fact, quite wrong.   The Operative Masons were originally " The Companions "
of the 17th Nome of Upper Egypt, and were
Stellar Cult people ; probably some later generations adopted the Solar Cult, and thus mixed the
signs, but retained the true and original Ritual.
Some of the exponents of Operative Masonry say
that the Swastika is a Symbol of Axial Rotation,
and refers to the Pole Star and the rotation of the
Great Bear around it ; that it symbolizes the Great
Ruler of the Universe, who alone was stationary
and stable as the North Star, while all the rest
of the universe revolves around Him !

   This Symbol or Sign does not mean anything of
the kind.   It is a pure theory without any foundation in fact, except imagination, and I challenge
any Operative Mason to bring forward any facts
to prove and support their theory.

   In its original form the Swastika is a symbol
of the Four Quarters of Heaven.   It is a typical
figure of the Heaven that was founded on the

Four corners, "according to the measure of a man" (Rev. xxi. 17), and its origin was derived from the human figure. The proof of this was found in a Prehistoric Grave at Nagada, in Egypt. On one of the seal Cylinders we have depicted the primitive form, which was two human figures crossed. These figures are depicted as in Fig. 59. The four limbs, which eventually became the four feet, or four legs, were at first the two arms and two legs of the human figure. This is the divine man whose image was extended

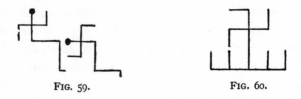

FIG. 59.   FIG. 60.

crosswise on the universe as a type of creation, and who was Atum in the character of Iu, the Son, in the early Solar Cult. From these two figures other two figures were blended, representing there-from the Four Quarters of Heaven. As proof of this there is still to be seen a stone at Meigle, in Perthshire, with these four figures forming a Swastika, a photograph of which is given in " Signs and Symbols of Primordial Man." Each quarter was given, or assigned, to one of the four Brothers of Horus, who were the four attributes representing the four Supports of Heaven. If further proof be necessary, it may be found in the Ancient Mexican Calendar, in the form of the Swastika. On each arm of this is the name of the four Brothers of Horus, who were the four Supports of Heaven, when first depicted in the form of a Square, in Primary Solar Cult, or when Heaven was first divided into four quarters by our old Brothers, who were the Astro-Mythologists of old Egypt.

Another form of the Swastika which is found in many countries, India and Cornwall especially, is Fig. 60, which is another portrayal of the form we find in Mexico. The four lines or uprights, having the same length as each arm, represent the four supports, or Brothers of Horus, as the four supports of the four quarters, which proves the truth of this decipherment.

This Triangle, then, with the Swastika in the centre is a Symbol for Horus, God of the Four Quarters, or God of the Double Horizon, and has nothing to do with the symbolism of God of the North Pole, or of axial rotation, as the Operative Masons explain. I have brought forward some existing proofs which cannot, I think, leave any doubt in your minds. I have explained this Symbol fully, because it is so frequently found in Wales, which was one of the last places, if not the last place, where the Druids existed in these Isles, where they lived and practised the old Solar Cult they had brought with them from Egypt.

Another form or Symbol for Heaven was the square, Fig. 61. The reason being that the Egyptians, in their progressive evolution from the division of Heaven into North and South, now added East and West, thus forming the Heavens into four Quarters, or a Square, by means of the Swastika figure. As already shown, there were two human figures, Right and Left, so they formed a Right and Left Swastika, as Figs. 62 and 63.

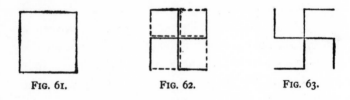

| FIG. 61. | FIG. 62. | FIG. 63. |

They crossed the two human figures, and if these two Swastikas be crossed they form a perfect Square, with four Quarters.

In India and other places, where we find the early Solar Cult existing, these two Swastikas are frequently found together as Right and Left. As by a Square they portrayed the Heavens, so by another Square they depicted the Earth. Thus, placing the two squares end to end, we arrive at the form in which all their Temples were built and are built, after the primary Circular

form had been given up. They placed a
treble cube in the centre to mark the division
between Heaven and Earth. On the top of the
Cube was a circle of gold, within this the Sacred
Triangle, with Ideographic Symbols at each corner,
signifying the names of the Primary Trinity, or
the Three Grand Originals, which all Royal Arch
Masons will recognize (see Fig. 64). This
double square end to end is the true form of our
Lodges, and the above is the reason why we have
them in this form, and also the reason why the

FIG. 64.   FIG. 65.

R.A.M.'s have the Cube in the centre and why
the Irish Masons still have " the Cube " in the
Centre of their Lodge. Originally these two
degrees were one.

One of the most interesting Symbols is the
Circle with a point in the centre (Fig. 65). For
the original of this we must return to the old wise
Brothers of Egypt ; the Mystery Teachers of the
Stellar Cult, although it was afterwards brought on
in the Solar, who had worked out the whole of
these Astronomical observations. It was previously

stated that the Pole Star North was symbolized by the one All-seeing Eye, also called the Great Judge of All ; also that the dot or Star at the summit of a Cone, or Triangle, was the Ideograph for Horus, God of the Pole Star North.   The point in the centre of a Circle is equal to the point at the top of the Triangle, and this Glyph is equivalent to the Eye ; the two are synonymous.   In this circle of the Pole Star there were seven attributes, called the Seven Glorious Ones, grouped together in the constellation of the Lesser Bear, revolving around the Most High, the Great Judge, the " All-seeing Eye," symbolized by the Pole Star, which was the centre of the circumpolar enclosure of Heaven, or Paradise, situated at the North.   The Eye, or this dot, or Pole Star, in the centre of the circle, therefore, became a Symbol or type of the eternal, because, apparently, it never changed with time.   It was the earliest type of the supreme intelligence which gave the Law, which was unerring, just, and true, and it became a standpoint in the heavens for the mind of man to rest on at the centre, and radiate to the circumference—a point within a circle from which a M.M. could not err.   It was a type or Symbol of the Just One, or the Just God, who gave the law, the Great Architect of the Universe, just and unerring.   We have made a bad innovation in our Ritual, because this was not the place where one learnt the secrets of a M.M., and this has been done, apparently, because the true gnosis of the Ancient Ritual of Egypt was not known to those who compiled our Ritual in its present form.

The old Egyptians formed an Ideographic Symbol called Amenta to teach the Mysteries, and it was here, in Amenta, that one learnt the true secrets of a M.M. In the 18° there is a room corresponding to this of the old Egyptians. You have been told that you travelled from the East to the West to learn the genuine secrets. That is so ; there you entered the Amenta in the West, travelled back to the East, and came out with all the true and genuine secrets of a M.M. This point within the circle was their circumpolar Paradise or Heaven, where you will all be received in spirit form after this earthly life, but you must possess all the secrets and passwords before you can enter there, according to the Egyptian Wisdom, and these were learnt in Amenta.

The Gavel (Fig. 12), the emblem or symbol of the W.M., is a Symbol of Power and Might, and its associations are very important. It was the original sacred sign used amongst primitive man, and originated with the little Pygmy in Africa. This, their sacred sign, is found in many countries, including Wales, Cornwall, France, America, and in Asia. Originally it was just three sticks crossed as in Fig. 10. Amongst the little

Pygmies it means "The Great One," "The Chief." If we trace the development of this to our present day we find three distinct evolutions of it. Amongst some of the Nilotic Negroes, who followed the Pygmy all over the world, and who are a higher developed type of man, they converted this Symbol into a double cross by placing the two sticks in a different way, as in Fig. 11. It is used by these Totemic people as one of their most sacred signs, and has been adopted by those who followed, down to our present Christian and other

FIG. 66.   FIG. 67.

Cults, as one of their sacred signs. It is used by our Brothers of the Higher Degrees. Amongst the Stellar Cult people it was carried on and used in its original form (Fig. 10), and is an Egyptian Ideograph for Amsu—i.e. the first name given to the risen Horus ; or, as Christians would say, the Risen Christ. . In a later period we have another symbol added to this, namely, the Egyptian Ru (see Figs. 66 and 67), which represents the mouth of a fish, and is an Ideograph for " An." It is the symbol which represents the giving birth to water as the Life of the World, and the Saviour who comes to Egypt by water, as the water of the inundation, or overflow of the Nile. When the ground was parched and dry, the overflow of the inundation occurred, and thus brought life, gladness, and plenty to all those who depended on the fructification of the soil, cultivated to maintain life, representing symbolically " The Water of Life," " The Saviour of Life," etc., and in conjunction with Fig. 10 would represent originally the Great One, the Great Saviour of Life, on which all must depend.   Various forms of this Symbol are to

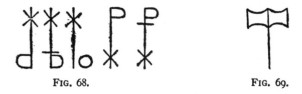

FIG. 68.   FIG. 69.

be found in Wales, Devon, and Cornwall, and in other countries ; some of these forms are as Fig. 68, but all have the same origin and meaning.

When stones took the place of sticks, and the knowledge of hafting had been attained—first amongst the Nilotic Negroes—some of these Nilotic Negroes represented this sign by a stone axe, or double-headed hammer, as in Fig. 69, to represent the Great One, the Great Prince. This became of great importance, and amongst some tribes a special hut was built for it. The Priest

and Great Chief were the only people allowed to
see it. This custom is still extant amongst the
Nilotic Negroes in Africa. I give here two copper
sacred axes which originally belonged to two native
chiefs or priests on the West Coast of Africa (A
and B) ; also some ancient sacred copper axes of

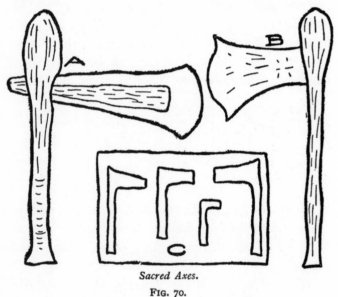

Sacred Axes.
FIG. 70.

the Egyptians '(c). In the Stellar Cult it
became one of the Symbols representing Horus.
" The Great Chief of the Hammer " was one of
his names ; " The Cleaver of the Way," " The
God of the Double Power, or Double Equinox,"
were other names by which he was known.

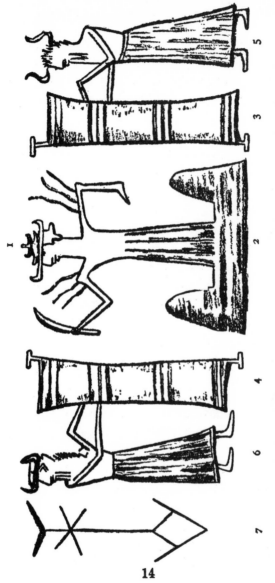

Shamash of the Chaldeans, Babylonians, and Assyrians, otherwise Atum-Iu of the Egyptians.

FIG. 71.

Perhaps the most important portrayal of this Symbol which can be found anywhere is that depicted on a Chaldean intaglio of green jasper in the Louvre, Paris, because it proves so much when correctly deciphered. See Fig. 71. It shows that : 1, it has been carried on from the Stellar into the Solar Cult in its primitive form ; 2, that in each case it identifies the same God under different Cults and different names ; 3, it also shows that the Chaldeans, Babylonians, and Assyrians obtained their cult from the Egyptians—all this is very important ; and 4, we find the same Symbol depicted in some churches in the West of England, especially in Cornwall, identically the same as is found on this intaglio. In the centre (1) we see depicted " Shamash "—their God—as rising from the under-world through the Eastern Gate (2)— that is in the morning—the Eastern Horizon. He is depicted between the Egyptian Hieroglyphic for the Horizon (2), which is contained between the two Pillars or Poles of North and South (3 and 4), which are supported by Hu and Sa (5 and 6)—these are attributes. Hu denotes matter. Sa signifies Spirit— i.e. the creation in blood and Spirit. The two Pillars North and South denote that it is the God of the North and South, as well as now East and West—the God of the Four Quarters. On the

left side of this picture we have the Sacred Signs
and Symbols (7), brought on from the Stellar Cult,
giving the Ideograph, which enables us to decipher
and interpret the meaning of the picture.   It will
be noticed that all the figures as here portrayed
are looking at the sacred name for the Risen
Lord (7).   This Symbol is interesting.   I have
already mentioned that the sign, Fig. 10, is the
Ideograph for Amsu in the Stellar Cult ;   the
Risen Horus, or Horus in Spiritual form.   This
is the principal part of the Symbol.   At the bottom

FIG. 72.   FIG. 73.

of this sign we have the Symbol Fig. 72, which,
in sign language, reads " He descended."   At the
top you have the Symbol Fig. 73, which, in
sign language, reads " He ascended."   The God,
as seen here, is issuing in the morning from the
under-world ; it is the Risen Horus—Amsu, of
the Stellar Cult, brought on into the earliest Solar.
One arm is raised, the right, free and uplifted
with the Flail in his hand, a Symbol of Power,
Majesty, and Might.   The other arm is not yet
free, the left.   He wears the Double Crown, Earthly

and Spiritual.   The three rays of light, seen on each arm, Fig. 74, denote his spiritual form, and give also the Ideograph for his name as that of Atum-Iu—the first God of the Solar Cult. Therefore, this figure is the first God of the Solar Cult, Atum-Iu, as the symbols prove, and is the same God Amsu-Horus brought on from the Stellar, and has the same Ideograph for his name. Here we have positive proof that the Chaldean, Babylonian, and Assyrian God, Shamash, is the Great God of the Double Horizon, or Double

FIG. 74.   FIG. 75.

Equinox of the Egyptians, Atum-Iu in the earliest Solar, Amsu-Horus in the Stellar, the Ihuh of the Hebrews, Tandayudhaswami of the Hindoos, and the Iu of the Welsh Druids.   This Sign and Symbol, Fig. 75, you will find depicted on the stone walls of many old churches in the West of England, and the interpretation here is that it represents Christ in His Spiritual form in the Christian Cult.   All one and the same Great God from the old Stellar to this day.

The Cult of Horus of the Double Horizon is

very important in tracing the evolution of religious conceptions and beliefs, as it gives the key to unlock the mysteries of the past. The Sphinx was cut out of the solid rock as an Ideographic Symbol to represent the passage of Horus from one Horizon to the other—symbolical, therefore, of Horus of the Double Horizon or Double Equinox, an early Solar Symbol and not Stellar. Thus these Signs and Symbols, with their true interpretation, will assist us to understand their true import, from the time they originally came into being down to the present, and why our old Brothers used them as representative Sacred Signs and Symbols in their Sign Language.

In the form of the Axe, from the Stellar it was brought on in the Solar Cult as one of the Symbols to represent the Great God Ptah ; the Great Architect of the Universe was one of his names, but he was also called the Great Chief of the Hammer (see Ritual of Ancient Egypt). Figs. 76, 77, and 78 represent the God of the Axe in three forms. Fig. 76 represents Ramman, the God of the Axe of the Susians. The horns here signify Solar Descent. The hair and features are those of " The Suk " of Africa. The Axe denotes that he is " The God of the Axe," " The Cleaver of the Way "—i.e. the Egyptian Horus of the Double Horizon or Double Equinox. The Three Rods or Rays of Light denote his name as that of Iu or Iau. He is therefore the Atum-Iu of the Egyptians. He is supported by his Four Brothers

Ramman, God of the Axe of the Susians.
FIG. 76.

—i.e. the Four Brothers or Children of Horus here portrayed in human form for the first time, as in the Stellar Cult these were represented by

Ramman, God of the Axe of the Chaldeans.
FIG. 77.

Zootypes : Man, Lion, Ox, and Eagle. The hair and features of these are the same as those of the " Suk " of Africa, from whom they descended.

Fig. 77 represents Ramman, God of the Axe of the Chaldeans. We have here a different type of man from the Ramman-Susian ; he wears a " conical hat and long robe," and his hair and features show a later type of evolution ; yet we find that he is also God of the Axe ; the interpretation of all the Symbols portrayed here proves that these people had the same Cult or religion. Ramman, the central figure, is shown as coming forth from the under-world, one foot on the mount of the Eastern Horizon ; above, we have portrayed two Pillars, North and South, and two Horizons, East and West, with the Sun depicted as rising and setting in each. Therefore God of the North and South, and God of the East and West. Below this we have, on the left, the Ideograph " He ascended " or " He has risen," and on the right we have the Star with eight rays, with the centre, which is a Symbol or Ideograph for the Chief or Great One as the 8th—i.e. 7 + 1, which was Stellar and Luna first, and the earliest Solar form before Ptah, who had the Cycle of 9. Below we see the under-world depicted with the Solar orb traversing it. This is Atum-Iu, God of the Double Equinox or Double Horizon of Egypt, the same as we have depicted with the other Gods.

In Fig. 78, representing the Mexican God
of the Axe, Tepoxtecatl, it will be seen that the
Symbolism in all is identically the same, and proves

Tepoxtecatl, God of the Axe of the Mexicans.
FIG. 78.

that all these old Stellar, or Solar, Cult people
originated and came from Egypt. These Cults
were carried out of Egypt by our old Brothers
to many parts of the world, and the remains of

these found at the present day demonstrate my claims as to the origin and evolution of the human race. It proves that our Brotherhood originated from the old Mystery Teachers of Egypt ; the proofs brought forward are irrefutable, both as regards the Origin and Evolution of Man and the Origin of our Brotherhood. In this case, however, it will be seen how ancient these people were. The Axe here is made of stone, and not metal.

The proofs of these things are to be found all over the world where these old Stellar and Solar Cult people lived. Many stones and buildings delineating the single or double Axe are to be seen in this country in Devon, Cornwall, in the Dolmens in Brittany, in Temples in America, and other parts of the world. At Knossos Evans found a Temple in the form of a double square, with three cubes in the centre, one surmounting the other, with this axe Ideograph on each, representing figuratively the Great One of the North —i.e. Horus ; the Great One of the South—i.e. Set ; the Great One of the Centre—i.e. Shu—the three Grand Originals, as in Fig. 4.

It will thus be seen that the symbol of the Axe, or gavel, has been handed down from the remotest antiquity, but the symbolism has not changed through all the evolutions of the human race. The few Symbols dealt with above go to show :—

1. That our old Brothers believed in one Great God, the Great Architect of the Universe.

2. That through all the various Cults that have succeeded the one to the other, up to the present day, it has always been the same God—the same Great Architect of the Universe.

3. That the use of different names during the evolution of the different races of mankind does not alter the Spiritual facts ; that the same Signs and Symbols, representing the G.A. of the U. and His attributes, have been used from the first to the last, under whatever name, and these are numerous. I have found some 1,500, and there are probably more.

It is interesting to understand why these Symbols and Signs are found in many parts of the world at the present day, and still used, not only by us, but some by the Hebrews, some by the Hindoos, many by the Chinese, Japanese, and others found amongst the Totemic peoples in many places in the world. Without knowing the Astro-Mythology and Eschatology, and Ritual of Ancient Egypt, we can never understand their meaning, or decipherment, or give a true explanation of what these old Signs and Symbols are. One can only guess, and give theories, which nine times out of ten are incorrect. It must be acknowledged that all these could not have been developed by several peoples—in many places in the earth, separately or independently ; they are too universal. There must have been one common centre. There was, and that was old Egypt. From Egypt, or along the Valley of the Nile, man originated, and spread throughout this earth. In old Egypt he began to grow in stature and knowledge, and from primitive faith man developed the highest religious doctrines. At first he had not the language as we have now ; many of his ideas were expressed in Signs and Symbols, and it is clearly and distinctly evident that these were used by these old Mystery Teachers to represent the Great Architect of the Universe, and His various attributes, and the doctrines of final things, when they had no language of words to express their thoughts as we have now.

As the old Egyptians progressed in knowledge and wisdom, so exodes left and went to most parts of the world—at least, the Stellar Cult people did —and many are extant at the present day, practising and believing in the old Stellar doctrine. From the Stellar they developed into a higher evolution—the so-called Solar Cult—and these went to India, nearly all over Europe, landed at Yucatan in Central America, and travelled down as far as Peru. They were called the Incas there ; here in Europe we called them the Druids. The Hindoos were an early exodus of these. The Hebrews or Jews were also an early Solar exodus.

We have in our forms and ceremonies, Signs and Symbols, the cult of these old Wise Men of Egypt, and it is not difficult to trace back how we came, and how all our Signs and Symbols have been brought on. We must not think, as some people do, that they worshipped these Signs and Symbols, because they did not ; we will take as an instance this so-called Idol, Tandayudhaswami, " if this was a Figure or Symbol of the Great God Atum," as Iu, it must have been Atum they worshipped and not the Symbol.

The old faith has never died, and we Freemasons have it in the purest form, with the additions which indicate the progress of humanity. Although we use the old Signs and Symbols as ancient types, we have replaced these by a language unknown to our old Brotherhood, in which we have developed a higher Spiritual terminology.

It is only within the last few years we have been able to read the Hieroglyphics. Even now we have very few students who can read and understand their ancient Astro-Mythology, and the evolution from this into their Eschatology, or their doctrine of final things. No country has yet attained again that high state of knowledge of Astronomy and Mathematics that these old Mystery Teachers possessed. They kept their wisdom to one class—these in Egyptian were called the " Hir-

Seshta," the Mystery Teachers, their High Priests —and much of their knowledge was communicated in sign language. Their Sacred Signs and Symbols were those they reverenced and treasured mostly ; hence, from one cult these were brought on into the next, sometimes altered somewhat, either added to, or something taken from, to mark the progress of the evolution of humanity. These things can still be traced with unerring fidelity by those who read the writings on the wall—up to our present generation. All the faiths and cults at the present day can be traced back to old Egypt and nowhere else. It is an object-lesson to remind us that without the belief in the Divine Creator our Brotherhood could not remain cemented together. That is the one point above all others we believe in, although under different terminology, and He is always The One and For Ever the Same Divine Master, under whatever Signs or Symbols portrayed.

X

SOME PROOFS THAT FREEMASONRY IS PART OF THE ESCHATOLOGY OF THE ANCIENT EGYPTIANS

A Lecture delivered before the Humber Installed Masters'
Lodge, No. 2494, Hull, on November 7, 1913.

As you are well aware, of late years more especially, many students of Freemasonry have arrived at the conclusion that our Brotherhood must have originated far away back in past ages, because, since the facilities of inter-communication have become so easy, many who have travelled much have found in India, China, Japan, Africa, America, and other places, many of our sacred Signs and Symbols connected with the religious rites and ceremonies of the old inhabitants of those places, but have been unable to form any definite conclusions as to the why and wherefore. Past and present writers on Freemasonry have ignored all the origins of our Signs and Symbols, because they were, and are, unacquainted with the key to unlock the Mystery, and there are no

writings, or history, to help them that they can
read. ` But the origin of Freemasonry dates back
to the time when these Signs and Symbols were
first formed—six hundred thousand years ago is a
low estimate.

One of the earliest Temples of the old Brotherhood was established at Edfu, in Egypt, by the
Priests of the Stellar Cult. The old Totemic
and Hero-Cult Nilotic Negroes had, through evolution, established this cult, with its beginnings of
the doctrine of final things. They came up from
the south of the Nile Valley, where they had
already formed a secret society, calling themselves
" the followers of Horus " (or " the blacksmiths "). Descendants of these still exist in the
Nile Valley—" the Kaverondo." They brought
with them the knowledge of working in metals
and of brickmaking and building. The Gemi tribe
of these were the religious part of this secret
society, learned already, in astronomical observations and secret doctrines.

Horus, their Great Chief in Hero-Cult, was now
symbolized as " The Great God of the North and
South." Another of his titles was " The Chief
Artificer in Metals." " The Great Chief of the
Hammer " and many other titles were gradually
added as evolution progressed for the G.G. of
the U. (We have substituted T.C. for Horus—
Behutet—which latter was the Egyptian word for

the first artificer in metals.) These people established the city of Edfu as their centre, and built
Temples for the G.A.U. throughout Egypt, after
driving out or exterminating the Pygmy and
Masaba Negroes, the original inhabitants (see
" Origin and Evolution of Primordial Man ").
Thus a brotherhood in two phases was established, the first being a religious sect, with their
Priests, having the astronomical and other knowledge ; and the second being the Builders, skilled
as artificers and brickmakers. Combined, these
were called the Mesniti or Mesintu, or the followers
of Horus, only another name, as the Christians
are called the followers of Christ. From the
Ritual of Ancient Egypt, still extant, we find that
the old Priests founded and established the Seven
Mysteries, afterwards called the Lesser Mysteries,
based upon Astro-Mythology. These were afterwards increased to twelve in the Stellar Cult.
Of these, the first two were communicated to " the
Builders," who were now established in the seventeenth Nome of Upper Egypt. The Ari by name,
and those who were initiated into the First and
Second Mysteries, were taken for the builders of
their Temples.

These Builders were divided into Craftsmen
and Companions, and a Priest was placed over
them, and was initiated into the Third Mystery,
but he was not Operative. These Builders of the

15

Temples were so initiated because the Priests
wished to keep the secrets of the Temples, and no
others were ever allowed to build or repair their
sacred places during the Stellar Cult. These were
the original Operative Masons, the descendants
of whom still exist, and, although these now have
a division of so-called seven degrees, which they,
constructed out of the two mysteries, the original
was simply the First and Second Mysteries.   I
think you will see that I am correct when I say
that they are still divided into two moieties, " The
Blue " and " The Red," also " The first four
Degrees " work with their hands, the others " work
with their heads "—these are known by the two
names of Craftsmen and Companions—so really
the old division is still kept. The Sacred Signs
and Symbols founded and established by the
learned priesthood had, however, another meaning
and definition from that which the Operatives were
taught—" A Sign Language " of their own, and
in a most profound and religious sense, which
was only known to the religious brotherhood, or
their Priests, and not to the Builders. It was from
these learned Priests that Speculative Masonry took
its origin. Thus you will see the origin of the so-
called Operative and Speculative Masons, of which
Anderson and all those Masonic writers who have
followed him, were ignorant. I do not propose
to follow the evolution of the Operative Masons

now, although I am well acquainted with all, and could prove from photographs of some of the Humboldt Fragments that they had their workings in Central America the same as they have here.

During the Stellar Cult, which lasted about three hundred thousand years, the Old Egyptians attained a high state of knowledge, and sent colonies nearly all over the world ; the proof of this can be demonstrated by the remains of their old Temples which have been found, and also their skeletons buried in the thrice bent position, and with a definite class of implements buried with them. Proof of this is afforded by the translation of an inscription found at Dendera, which also goes to show how far advanced were the Stellar Cult people in arts and writings. The literal translation as the Egyptian words stand is :—

" Was found foundation great in Dendera, in writings old in rolls of kids in the time of the followers of Horus, was found between the wall of brick of the South part in the reign of the King of the Sun-beloved the son of Sun Lord of diadems Phiops."

This, when translated into modern English, would read : " That in the great foundation, in Dendera, between the walls of brick at the Southern part of the Temple, were found decayed rolls of parchment with writings thereon of the followers of Horus."

I bring forward this evidence that you may not be carried away by enthusiasm, which some Brethren declare I am exceedingly liable to in my own case, and that I put forward theories instead of facts. But let me assure you that I belong to an honourable profession where we are trained to think, reason, and sift the objective and subjective proofs to the bottom. The facts I lay before you are objective and capable of proof.

The Stellar Cult was followed by the Lunar, and then by the Solar, and finally by the Christian doctrines. At the time of the zenith of the Solar Cult, at the latest, it is certain that they had established ten more Mysteries, called the Greater Mysteries, and worked out their Eschatology, or doctrine of final things, and had established their Sign Language and rituals for these. I do not know how, or why, all these have been divided up into thirty-three degrees as we have done, because in all, the Stellar and Solar added together, I can only make twenty-two. In the Stellar there were seven at first, afterwards five more were added.[1] In the Solar ten more were added, but many of these were a different form of the Stellar. It was an attempt to blot out the former cult, but at the

[1] The Stellar Mysteries were, however, afterwards subdivided into twenty-four.

same time really bringing it on under a new name, changing the original names by substituting others. We in this Lodge have the old Stellar Mysteries, but when you come to the eighteenth degree and upwards, you change into the Solar with much mixture of the Stellar, and some of the Christian added, so you may be quite certain that ours up to the R.A. are the Stellar or oldest, and, although our traditional history only dates from Solomon's Temple, you can be certain that it existed thousands of years before the time of Solomon.

Let me here explain how you may always still distinguish the old Stellar Cult buildings from the Solar, and those which followed after. Wherever you find the remains of two circles, these were Stellar Cult Temples. They were built with twelve monoliths, or twelve pillars for each circle, and were pre-zodiacal, indicating the divisions of heaven into twelve divisions of the North and twelve divisions of the South ; these were two separate circles. The Solar Cult people always built with three circles (or in the form of a Double Square), one representing the North and another the South. The third was placed between, the two circles bisecting each other like links in a chain. These divided heaven into thirty-six divisions. I do not mean you to understand that only twelve stones were used in building each Temple. There were as many used as in other

erections, but there were twelve monoliths, or
pillars of special import. These were placed outside the walls, sometimes inside the Temple.

The primary formation of the Temples was
round, and sometimes two were built together,
one North and one South. These were built when
Set was Primary God of the South. An example
of one of these can still be seen at Peking ; it
is there called The Temple of Heaven, the oldest
form found in China. Another exists in Central
America, known as the Temple of Set, at Tepe-
yollott, Mexico, as depicted in the Borgian Codex.
The formation of this Temple is round, and on
the top is one of the Symbols or Ideographic
names of Set—the God of the South. These two
Temples—one from China and the other from
Mexico—show that the first form of the Temples
was round, and that they were dedicated to Set—
the God of the South Pole, previous to Horus—the
God of the North. They also show how widely
distributed these old Primary Stellar Mythos
people were, and that the cult was one and the
same all over the world at this time. From evidences contained in the Ritual, this Primary
Cult lasted about fifty-two thousand years before
the change to the North took place. Disbelievers
should estimate how long it must have taken man
to migrate these great distances, found communities, and erect Temples. Curiously enough, the

Symbol or Ideograph for the name of Set is still
used on some of the Government stamps and
official paper of some of the South American
States.   In this country we now call it the Dunce's
Cap, or Fool's Cap.

The Chinese were Stellar Cult people originally,
but now there is much mixture of the Solar Cult
with these.   The reason why they built in these
two circles was because they divided the heavens
into two divisions of North and South, portrayed
as two circles, as I have already stated.   These
Temples therefore represented their circumpolar
paradise, within which " the house " of the G. A.
of the U. was situated.   Remains of these two
circles can be found in many parts of the world
where the old Stellar Cult people went.   In this
country I have recently examined some on Dart-
moor, Devonshire.   Of course, you would not expect
to find anything but remains here now.   We have
passed through several glacial epochs since these
were built, and they would be destroyed by the ice
and snow.   You will also find three circles in many
places.   These belong to the Solar Cult people.
You will find this fully set forth in the second
edition of " Signs and Symbols of Primordial
Man."

In these circular Temples the altar was circular,
and placed in the centre of the building.   There
were in the primary Temples five steps, afterwards

seven steps, leading up to this. In most cases the
Temple was open at the top to the vaults of heaven,
so that a " Plumb Line " might come straight
from the Pole Star to the central altar. The seven
steps represent in the Egyptian " The Khuti,"
or the seven Glorious Ones—attributes of the G. A.
of the U., whose house is situated within this circumpolar enclosure. They also represent the seven
Great Spirits—the seven Sciences—the seven Eyes
—and many other sevens of the Scriptures. The
twelve Camps, and the twelve Banners of the
Children of Israel represent the original characters
in the Stellar Astronomical Mythology, and were
given first to the twelve Thrones, or divisions of
heaven in the Stellar Cult, and in the Zodiac
in the Solar. Thus, at first, they represented
twelve Stellar Powers, and that is the reason we
find the twelve Stones in these Circles. The
original characters in the Astronomical Mythology that were given the twelve Thrones, or Camps,
with separate and distinctive Banners in Zootype
form, in Egyptian are Set, Horus, Shu, Hapi, Ap-
uat, Kabhsenuf, Amsta, Anup, Ptah, Atum, Sau,
and Hu. These were the Kamite originals, brought
on and converted into the Banners of the Twelve
Camps, or Tribes, of Israel. The four principal
Banners in the R.A.C., depicting the man, lion, ox,
and eagle, took their origin from the four Brothers
or Children of Horus. These are to be found

all over the world wherever the Stellar Cult existed, and appear under various names. The Temples which were built after these were in the form of the so-called " double square "—in the form of our Lodges—and all Temples throughout the world, after the circular, were in that form, which has been retained ever since.

Another distinctive character between the Stellar and Solar buildings was that all the old Stellar Cult people's buildings were Iconographic. By that I mean the G. A. of the U. and all His attributes were depicted on these Temples in a pre-human form—i.e. Zootype form. Men at this time had not yet learnt to portray the human form as human, and so these types were depicted as snakes, birds, and other Zootype forms. Whereas at the time of the Solar Cult all the attributes of the G. A. of the U. were portrayed in the human form. The transition stage was during the Lunar Cult. These are the differences which will enable you always to distinguish the one from the other, ever remembering that both built with Polygonal stones and monoliths. Another point I might mention is that the cement used by the old Stellar Cult people was much finer than that used by the Solar. Good examples of each are still extant in South Africa and Central and South America. The fineness of this cement has caused many writers and observers to state that there was no cement used ; but others, of more acute observation, discovered that there was a very fine cement, which was composed of granite very finely ground, or of the same material as the principal stones were composed of.

The Secrets of the Mysteries were to teach man how to live here on earth, how to die, and what he had to pass through after death before he could finally enter Paradise, founded on the belief of the death and disintegration of the Corpus, and the Resurrection of the Spiritual Body for eternity. The many eulogies that have been showered upon Sir Oliver Lodge and the Bishop of London, on account of their recent addresses, prove how very little is known of the Old Egyptian Eschatology. In neither of their addresses was there anything new. In fact, the beliefs they expressed are as old as the Pygmies, as I have proved these primitive people believed in a Supreme Being, an after life, and propitiating the Spirits of their departed friends, as well as the elemental powers. During the time that elapsed from the origin of these Pygmies to that grand evolution of Eschatology of the old Hir-Seshta, they had trained Spiritual Clairvoyants to undergo Hypnotism and communicate with departed spirits. This is still practised by some men of the present day, but it is not given to every one. In fact, very few have sufficient courage and patience to

attain the power, even if they have a good Spiritual
Clairvoyant as the connecting intermediary, which
is just as rare. Still, they do exist, and the laws
of this do not clash with " science or religion "
—in fact, you must not only " be religious," but
also " scientific " to attain this power in its desirable form. Having gained that power, most
secrets of the Celestial and Terrestrial worlds are
available, or anything else that is right for one
to learn. But there are many things beyond a
certain point which cannot be explained for want
of adequate language or word, and through lack
of corresponding Symbol. But, as in the Egyptian
Eschatology, it is possible to discover who are
amongst the " blest," and who " have failed to
be justified," and who have found that the balance,
Maat, has weighed against them. It was understood that " no bad people " on earth could ever
attain this knowledge. It was only " the good
people here " that have sufficient power to send
the earthly living Spirit into the Circumpolar Paradise situated at the North, and have communion
with the Blessed there ; to be " Maa-Kheru,"
to come in and go out, and to whom all doors are
open. The old High Priests of Egypt obtained
much of their knowledge in this way, but through
the past dark ages, since the downfall of the
Egyptian Empire, the secrets have been known
to only a very few. Scientists are now beginning

to regain some of these secrets, thinking it is a new phase in the further development of the human brain. But it is not ; it is old, and has been forgotten by the general masses of Scientists and Priests. But the Ritual of Ancient Egypt will give more knowledge on this subject than all the present Scientists and Divines combined would dare to give, even if they had the knowledge.

The wonderful manner in which these ancient ideas have been preserved and carried to distant parts of the world will be seen by a reference to Fig. 78, which represents Tepoxtecatl, the Mexican God of the Axe. From the Mendoza Codex, No. 13, we find that the Mexicans, when they began to spread beyond their Valley of Quauhnauac, made war on Tepoxtlan. They were told that this place was called " The Place of the Axe," and that Tepoxtecatl was the God of the Axe, a Great Seer of the Hammer. Fig. 78 is reproduced from the Mexican painting in the Biblioteca Nazionale, Florence, in which the Axe is depicted in two forms, one in his hand, a double axe, and a single axe in front of him. He wears the double crown, Earthly and Spiritual, and has the emblem of the God Iu supported by four pillars, representing the four brothers or Children of Horus ; the same is also symbolized on his banner.

Fig. 79 represents the God of the Axe from

Tinogasta, Argentina, called their Uracocha.   The
same God is portrayed on the Monolithic Gate at
Tiahuanaco, Bolivia, at the south end of the Lake
Titicaca.   Other names in South America, in

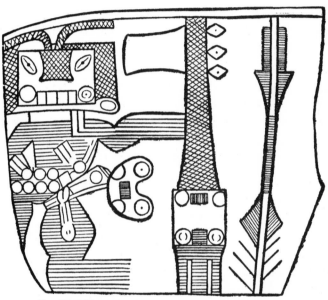

Con Tiesi Uracocha, God of the Axe, from Tinogasta.

FIG. 79.

different States, are Tonapa, Tarapaca, Irma, and
Iraya.   These were all during the Stellar Cult.   In
the Solar the name was Tachacamac, equal to Atum-
Iu ; the full name in the Stellar Cult was Con Tiesi

Uracocha.   In this symbol his name is portrayed by the two feathers on his head.   The Itheophallic Symbol, and Fan, denote a new life, the Spiritual. The Fan was used in the Egyptian Mysteries to signify a Spirit, and with the Itheophallic emblem denotes the Resurrection of the Spirit.   The Christian Copts (Priests) still use this emblem, but we have lost it.   The Axe is supported by the four Children of Horus, with the House of Heaven (also depicted on the Fan) and the House of Earth —i.e. The House of Earth and House of Eternity. Beneath are portrayed the two Poles or Pillars of the North and South, signifying that he is the God of the North and South.   On the extreme right is the emblem of Sovereignty, Power, and Might.

In Fig. 80 is a symbol of the God of the Axe from Tepozteco, now in the Museum Trocadero. The symbols on the front of the Conical Hat give his name as Iu, as also do the ear ornaments. The Masonic Apron which is here portrayed will be recognized quite readily.

As the latest confirmation that the origin of these symbols came from Mother Egypt, I here give some linear writing, or ancient script, found by Dr. Morgan on a tablet in Egypt, which has never before been translated.   I am pleased to have been able to accomplish this, and here give it for the first time since the destruction of Ancient

God of the Axe of the Toltec, from Tepozteco.

FIG. 80.

Egypt. The Script is reproduced in Fig. 81, and, reading from right to left, may be thus deciphered :—

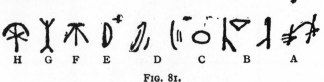

FIG. 81.

A It is written.
B Horus, God of the North and South.
C Saviour of the World.
D Beloved.
E Lord (or Son).
F Iu.
G He descended, He ascended.
H Amsu; the Risen Horus for Eternity.

Translated into the modern idiom, it would therefore read :—

" It is written Horus, God of the North and South, Saviour of the World, the beloved Son or Lord Iu. He descended ; He ascended. He is now Amsu, the risen Lord in Spirit form, and reigns for Eternity."

This form of writing is that which was used during the time they were converting the pure Hieroglyphic into Hieratic, which was a gradual change, and must have taken a considerable time. A and D are Hieratic, and others the pure old

Hieroglyphics. The sign B, the Ideograph for Horus, God of the North and South, was in this form used in the Stellar Cult only. Here we have the two Poles or Pillars of the North and South supported by Hu and Sa—the two supports, with the Ideograph Triangle for the name of Horus between the Pillars at the top.

There are not any symbols of the two Horizons here, because this was written during the Stellar Cult, and the two Horizons did not come into being until the early Solar Cult, when they changed Horus God of the North and South, into Atum-Iu, the God of the Double Horizon, East and West, and he became the God of the Four Quarters, in early Solar Cult in a different form from God of the North, South, East, and West of the Stellar. Still, it was the same god.

I do not think any further proof is necessary, to show the correctness of these statements, unless perhaps you would consider a quotation from the Ritual of Ancient Egypt necessary. In the XXX Ch Ritual occur these words : " Heart mine which is that of my Mother ; whole heart mine which was that of my coming on Earth. Let there be no estoppel against me through evidence, let no hindrance be made to me by the divine circle : fall through not against me in presence of him who is in the Balance. Let not those Ministers who deal with a man according to the course of his

16

life give a bad odour to my name. And lo! though he be buried in the deep, deep grave, and bowed down to the region of annihilation, he is glorified, then—lo, how great art Thou—The Triumphant One."

This shows and proves it was the Stellar Cult. "The Mother" it was, and not "The Father." The Father had not yet come into being—not until the Solar Cult. The Glorious Ones, or "the Divine Circle," were those attributes of Horus represented symbolically by the Stars of Ursa Minor. This text is very old, and there is one copy on a Scroll in the British Museum.

If we merely consider the tokens of recognition, the passwords, secret words, and the decorations of the Lodges, according to the degrees into which Modern Masonry is divided, we find that many of them are taken from the V. of the S.L., and are symbolical of events, real or imaginary, some of which are said to have taken place in those comparatively modern times which followed the decline and destruction of the old Egyptian Empire, and marked the commencement of the Christian Era, others as having occurred before the Christian Cult commenced, others at the building of King Solomon's Temple. All of which, some think, and have stated, have nothing to do with the religious Mysteries of the Egyptians that were in existence many hundreds of thousands of years before.

Where do those who positively affirm that all these have not been derived from the Egyptians suppose they originated? Whence did the above obtain them? Recent discoveries have proved beyond a doubt that all through Africa, Europe, Asia, America, and many of the Pacific Islands, during the Stellar period there was but this one religious cult practised, taught, and believed in by all. Their industries, arts, and sciences were common and universally the same. The Signs and Symbols that we use were theirs, as witnessed by these still found amongst the ruins.; and the centre of intellect, and origin, was Egyptian. I affirm from personal observations and study, and it is open to all students to confirm my observations and translations, that these Signs and Symbols still existing on the walls of Ancient Temples and ruined cities in Africa, Asia, Europe, and America, as well as many islands in the Pacific, are identical in every form and shape with those now used amongst the Brotherhood, and I further maintain that these translations of their Rituals, which we have now discovered and can read, are analogous to our own ; at the same time, I must say that many innovations have naturally been made, because it became necessary to replace those secrets that were lost, and also to meet the higher state of evolution which mankind has now reached.

I cannot now enter into the question of how,

when, and where these Symbols and Rituals first came to this country, but if you follow the progress and evolution of the human race, its migrations, arts, sciences, and religious cults, in the various waves of exodes from Egypt, the rise and fall of the different Empires that have taken place, the results and effects upon peoples that flourished in latitudes down to 50 degrees, by the Glacial Epoch recurring every 25,827 years—the destruction of the old Egyptian Empire over five thousand years ago, followed by fire, sword, and a dark and degenerate age of all that pertained to their old civilization—you will begin to understand a little, and when you consider how tenacious mankind is of the religious doctrines that they have been taught, and brought up in, by their fathers and mothers, you will understand that, in spite of all the persecution they were subjected to by the Roman Priesthood, there would be many in various countries who would secretly cling to and carry on their old beliefs.

Herodotus states that all the Zoroastrian, Dionysiac, Serapism (or Greek), Mithrasism, Samothracian, Pythagorean, and Eleusnian Mysteries were obtained from the Ancient Egyptians, and that most of these were initiated into these Mysteries by the Pelasgians, who stated that they were initiated into these Mysteries by the Egyptians. Then the Stellar Cult people travelled and settled in most parts of Africa, Asia, Europe, America, North and South, and many islands of the Pacific, and the Solar followed them into Asia, Europe, and some parts of America. The Chinese and most of the Japanese are still Stellar Cult people, but now much mixed with the Solar. The Druids, Incas, and Hindoos were all Solar Cult people. The Druids, or Culdees, existed here until quite a modern date, and then some of their Priests joined the Christian Church. The oldest churches in the West of England and other places bear witness of how they brought over some of their Sacred Signs and Symbols with them, introducing the same as Symbols of the new Cult.

During the dark and degenerate ages of nearly five thousand years, records were destroyed ; we have no history of the past hundreds of thousands of years of this world's existence. Socialism crept in after the dissensions amongst the Priests themselves, followed by fire and sword, and the destruction of literature, arts, and sciences followed. This has always been the history of past great nations. History repeats itself. But our Brotherhood has inherited a sacred legacy ; after being scattered over the face of the earth and water, we have come together again, in spite of the persecution of the Roman Priesthood, and it now rests with the Brotherhood throughout the world to say if we shall in the future establish that one human

Brotherhood as of old, founded on the belief of a Divine Creator, and an Eternal and Everlasting Spiritual Life hereafter, grasping the opportunity to consummate that which must be the dream of every Freemason ; or shall we, through dissension, apathy, and want of universal combination with our Brotherhood, further postpone it to future generations?

The past evolution of the history of the human race has been an object-lesson to remind us that, without the belief in the Divine Creator, our Brotherhood could not remain cemented together. That is, and must be, our object above all others, and although we find various terminology used for Him, under different organizations and in the various cults, as these have risen and been replaced by others, He is always "The One, and for ever the same Divine Master, under whatever Sign and Symbol—the Great Architect of the Universe."

Remember that, for Freemasonry to exist, there is no way of standing still—it must progress or it must fall ; the human intellect is again expanding after all the dark ages we have passed through, a dark and deep pit of ignorance, out of which we cannot be extricated except by the Egyptian ladder. With the example of a great universal past, we have the opportunity of making a great universal future Brotherhood, as of old. Grant that this may be speedily consummated.

XI

THE FOUR CARDINAL POINTS

As the Four Cardinal Points are brought into prominence in the various Masonic Degrees, and as many very erroneous ideas exist as to the origin and meaning of what is taught with regard to them, their real origin, meaning, interpretation, and symbolisms will be of interest here.

The full explanation necessitates reference to some of the decipherments I have already given to prove the association of the progressive evolutions of the human race, with regard to the Four Cardinal Points. The Old Mystery Teachers of Egypt mapped out, or divided, the Heavens first into two divisions, South and North. The " Points " being the two Pole Stars, resting on the Horizons, as seen in the centre of Africa, " Points which never changed with time," represented symbolically as Set and Horus, Twins of the Great Mother, " the Two Primary Gods," symbolized by two Poles or Pillars or two Eyes, and sometimes by two Circles. These also represented Light and

Darkness, also the two Seasons of the Old Egyptian Year. The old Egyptians first divided their year into (1) the Season of Summer Water, (2) the Season of Winter Drought. Also these were called the two original "Ancient Ones." It was at this time the two Cardinal Points—North and South=Set and Horus—"first came into being." The next phase was Heaven being divided into three divisions, or "triangular form," with the God Shu added to the two above, placed at the Equinox, forming the Primary Trinity.

These three represented the first three Sons, or Elementary Powers, born of the Great Mother, and symbolized in Egypt in one form by "The Water Cow," the Crocodile, and the Lion : representing (1) Light, (2) Darkness, (3) the breathing power, or Winds. Also they represented the three Seasons, into which the Egyptians had then divided their year—1. The water season, represented symbolically by Horus ; 2, the season of wind, or breath of life, and of the Equinoctial gales, by Shu ; 3, the season of Dryness and Drought, by Set ; called (1) the Water Season, (2) the Green Season, and (3) the Dry Season. The Signs and Symbols for which were (1) Water, (2) Growing Plants, (3) a Barn or Storehouse indicating that the harvest was gathered. The names in Egyptian for these Seasons are Se, Pir, Semon.

The three Seasons of four months led to the

circle of the Ecliptic being measured and divided into three parts, i.e. a Triangular division. The Egyptian month was divided into three weeks of ten days each, which obviously corresponded to the Heaven of the Triangle, the tripartite Ecliptic and the three Seasons of Egypt. Many other forms of the first three elementary spirits or attributes of the G.A.U. might be mentioned, but they do not concern us here.

In the next progressive evolution the Old Mystery Teachers divided Heaven into four Quarters, as a Square with four sides, in which may be traced " four houses." This division into four Quarters was first symbolized by a man and 'then by the crossing of two men, as is proved by the symbols found depicted in the tomb of Nagada (see Fig. 59). This was the origin of the Swastika, which proves this Sign and Symbol to be that of the four Quarters. At the Cardinal Points, North, South, East, and West, of which the latter two had " now come into existence," were stationed the four Brothers or Children of Horus, as the four supporters and protectors of the Four Cardinal Points, and the supporters and bearers of each Quarter. Therefore we find that " Two Cardinal Points, North and South " were first formed, or founded, many thousands of years before the other two, namely East and West. Now at each Cardinal Point one of the four Brothers of Horus was assigned a place. These are the children of Horus who stand on the Papyrus plant, or Lotus, born of water, in the new Kingdom that was founded for the Father by Horus the Son. Two of these children, Tuamutef and Kabhsenuf, are called the two fishes (Ritual, ch. 113), and elsewhere the followers of Horus are the fishers or fishermen. Horus was teacher of the Lesser Mysteries in his first advent, and teacher of the Greater Mysteries in his second advent. And this is the reason why we find Four Cardinal Points in the Stellar Cult, as well as in the Solar, although it has been often overlooked by Egyptologists. But when Shu " lifted up the Heavens " (which I have already explained), the Cardinal Points, East and West, were added to the attributes of Horus, as God of the East and West, as well as North and South, and the four Brothers were assigned to these points. These were called Brothers in the Stellar Cult and Children in the Solar. They were four out of the divine circle of twelve which was established first in the Stellar Cult, and in Ritual, ch. 30, they are referred to " as being on the side Lord of Horus," i.e. with him in his youth, or earthly career.

This refers to the resurrection as it was rendered in the Eschatology. Thus when Horus rose again upon the Mount, he was accompanied by

the Spirits of the Four Corners, or Cardinal
Points, with whom his fold was founded (Ritual,
ch. 97). These four being added to the three
Primary made up the Seven Great Spirits of the
Stellar Cult, called the " Khuti " or " Glorious
Ones." These seven were symbolized as
(1) Sebek-Horus, the Crocodile ; (2) Set, the
Water Bull ; (3) Shu, the Lion ; (4) Hapi, the
Ape ; (5) Tuamutef, the Jackal ; (6) Kabhsenuf,
the Hawk ; (7) Amsta, the Man. Thus we have
the three Primary in the Triangle and four in
the Square = the Seven Great Spirits of Heaven
and Earth. The new Heaven was thus established on the Four Quarters that were founded
upon the solstices and equinoxes, and

These four (1) Hapi, (2) Tuamutef, (3)
Kabhsenuf, and (4) Amsta, were stationed at the
Four Cardinal Points.

As Egyptian, they are four Great Spirits at the
four corners of the Mount of Heaven, and in
Revelation they are the " four angels standing at
the four corners of the Earth, holding the four
winds of the Earth (Rev. vii. 1). (See later
representation in Calendar wheel of Duran.) The
Kamite Four, reproduced in Revelation as the
four living creatures—the first creature like a
Lion, the second like a Calf, the third had the
head of a Man, and the fourth creature like a
flying Eagle (Rev. iv. 7)—these four, under

whatever names or forms, are the same, and their
duties are the same in whatever part of the world
found.   In their primary form they are " the four
living creatures " with the eyes, which as Egyptian
are Ape-headed, Jackal-headed, Bird-headed, and
Human-headed.

In a secondary phase they were given the human
figure, and both forms of the four are repeated in
the Revelation of John.   According to Revelation,
" the four living creatures " are full of eyes round
about and within, and they have no rest day and
night, as they are moving round for ever with
the sphere.   Being astronomical figures, the eyes
of these were the Stars.   In the Ritual, the four
are Eyes symbolically, or the stars of the Four
Quarters.

The vignette to Chapter 148 of Ritual portrays
them as the four Eyes, or guiding Stars, one to
each Quarter, North, South, East, and West.   They
are spoken of in the Ritual as the Divine Powers =
his children or brothers as the four supports of the
future Kingdom (Ritual, ch. 112) and the Four
Glorious Ones (Ritual, ch. 92).

The Egyptians now divided their year into four
Seasons, which would roughly correspond to our
Spring, Summer, Autumn, and Winter, represented
in one phase by the Symbolic Brothers—one for
each Season.

These four Brothers, or Children, of Horus, pro-

tectors of the Four Cardinal Points, and supporters
of the Four Quarters, are very important in helping
us to trace man and his cults throughout the world.
I am giving the decipherment of some of the
Signs and Symbols representing these, found in
various parts of the world, which have never been
deciphered before or interpreted by any one, so
that my readers will find it easier to understand

FIG. 82.

the mysteries of the past, and their connection
with "the Marchens," and the reasons for the
importance attached to the Four Cardinal Points
in Freemasonry.

The Egyptian Originals were the Elementary
Powers, or Spirits, in Totemic Sociology, divinized
in the Stellar Cult, and brought on in various forms
through the Lunar, Solar, and Christian doctrines.

Fig. 82 reproduced here, gives the Egyptian

symbolic representation, and is taken from Bunsen's Dictionary.

They represented " the Signs " for the Four Cardinal Points of Heaven in the division of four, as a square. Afterwards four Consorts were assigned to them, representing half cardinal points, or Heaven in the division of eight, in one form.

Amongst the Stellar and Solar Cult peoples throughout the world we find various names for these, *but their places and duties were always identical,* as may be seen and is proved by the following. The reason for the different symbolification in representation is because the " fauna " as models for Zootypes were different in each country.

Amongst the Mexicans these were called—

Name	Cardinal Points	Sign or Symbol	Colour	Name of Consorts
1. Tecptl	North	Flint Knife or Shell	White	Cipactli
2. Tochtli	South	Rabbit or Hare's Head	Yellow	Cozcaquanhtli
3. Acatl	East	A Reed or Cane growing in Water	Red	Michitzli
4. Calli	West	A House	Black	Ozomatli

Amongst the Mayas—

1. Zac-Bacab = The White Bacab who stood at the North.
2. Kan-Bacab = The Yellow Bacab who stood at the South.
3. Chac-Bacab = The Red Bacab who stood at the East.
4. Ek-Bacab   = The Black Bacab who stood at the West.

Amongst the Zapotecs—

1. Been		Ix
2. Eyanab	also	Kau
3. Ahbal		Muluc
4. Lamal		Canac

Amongst the Peruvians—

1. Manco	Consort	Occlo
2. Cachi		Huaco
3. Uchu		Cura
4. Auca		Raua

Amongst the Chaldeans the Four Principal Protecting Genii of the Human Race were—

1. Sed-Alep ir Kirul represented as a Bull with Human Face ;
2. Lamas a Nirgal represented as a Lion with Human Head ;
3. Ustur, after the Human likeness ;
4. Nattiz, with the head of an Eagle ;

and were said by Ezekiel to be the four Symbolic creatures which supported the Throne of Jehovah, in his visions by the River Chebar.

These four are known to the Hindoos as the four Maharajahs or Great Kings of the Dylam Cholans—

1. India—The King of Heaven in the East.
2. Konvera—The God of Wealth in the North.
3. Varouna—The God of Waters in the West.
4. Yama—The Judge of the Dead in the South.

Amongst the Chinese they represent the Four Quarters or the Four Great Powers or Mythical Mountains.

1. Tai-Tsong	=	East
2. Sigan-fou	=	West
3. Hou-Kowang	=	South
4. Chensi-si	=	North

Amongst the Bavili and Bimi—

1. Ibara ⎫
2. Edi ⎪
3. Oyekun ⎬ As the four supporters of Ifi, the Son of God.
4. Oz-be ⎭

Amongst the Yoruba—

1. Ogun   = North = Red   ⎫
2. Shango = West   = Black   ⎪ These are the
3. Edgu   = East   = Yellow or Green ⎬ Four Odus of
4. Oshalla = South = White   ⎭ the Yorubas.

Other names on the West Coast of Africa are—

1. Edgu   = East   = Yellow or Green
2. Shamgo = West   = Black
3. Obatalla = South = White
4. Ogun   = North = Red

The Symbols or Signs of the Four Cardinal Points of the world as a Square, or four quarters, are found depicted in other forms as follows :—
Arranged as the Four Chief Odus amongst the Yoruba—

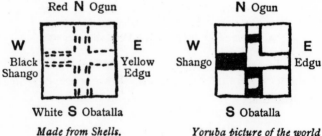

Red **N** Ogun

W   **E**
Black   Yellow
Shango   Edgu

White **S** Obatalla

Made from Shells.

N Ogun

W   **E**
Shango   Edgu

S Obatalla

*Yoruba picture of the world
by barked sticks.*

Pueblo Indian picture of the world in four quarters or divisions illustrated by barked sticks—

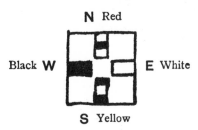

The Koreans depicted the Sign and Symbol of Heaven in a Square, and the Four Cardinal Points or divisions of Heaven in four quarters. Barked sticks—four sticks of equal length—form the square, and four sticks of equal length the centre arms. From the centre arm, the one representing the East, they removed all the bark, so that it was white ; from the one representing the West none of the bark was removed. The one representing the North had all removed but one piece in the centre, and in the South the bark was removed from the centre, leaving the bark at the two ends.

The Korean.

17

Amongst the Mopi their names were—

Gala	=	East
Sala	=	West
Arba	=	North
Nika	=	South

Amongst the Mandes—

Saga-djigi
Tulluguri
Kunato
Fianto

Amongst the Hebrews—

1. Man
2. Lion
3. Ox
4. Eagle

} The Four Standards of the Children of Israel as used amongst R.A.M.'s.

Amongst the Christians—

1. St. Matthew	Man	Egyptian	Man
2. St. Mark	Lion	„	Ape
3. St. Luke	Ox	„	Jackal
4. St. John	Eagle	„	Eagle

Revelation iv. 6 : " And in the midst of the Throne and round about the Throne were four beasts, full of eyes before and behind. The first was like a Lion. The second was like a Calf. The third had the face of a Man. The fourth was like a flying Eagle." (Plate D.)

Plate E here reproduced, a facsimile of Plate '44 Fejervary Codex, portrays the original so-called Maltese Cross of the 18º and 30º. Although the

PLATE D.—*The Four Evangelists, SS. Matthew, Mark, Luke, and John, depicted in Christian Symbolism as Man, Lion, Ox, and Eagle.*

PLATE E.—*The Risen Horus and his Four Brothers.*
(From the Fejervary Codex.)

To face p. 243.

Brothers of this degree do not know it, here is the original, and I now restore it to them. In the centre there is a square representing Heaven as a Square, with Horus as Amsu, or the risen Horus as God of the four quarters, as the central figure. Surrounding this figure there are the *four supports* represented by four Trees, one in each " arm," and in each one of these arms is one of the four Brothers of Horus, with his Consort supporting in Sign Language. Between each " arm " there is a " loop "; at the upper part of the " loop " is the name or Zootype form, or Symbol, for the name of each Brother. The Symbol is placed in the centre of the body of a bird (Eagle), proving this to be an " attribute " of the God Horus.

All are looking at the central figure, i.e. Horus as Amsu in Spirit, the Risen Christ, as the Christians would say.

In Sign Language we have here typically portrayed the risen Horus and his four Brothers, the latter as supporters of the Four Cardinal Points representing the attributes of Horus supporting the new Heaven founded on his second advent or resurrection.

Again, this is depicted by a bird (Eagle—Symbol for Horus) on the top of each Tree or Pillar, which is supported as here portrayed with the Brothers and their Consorts, an original " Stellar " form taken alone.

The Glyphs which tell you, and assign to each, the duties or attributes of these brothers, are shown between the "Arms" of the Cross and the "Loops," and are identical with the old Egyptian, as stated in the Ritual of Egypt. On the Loops there are 12 dots or small circles ◯ on each side, representing the 12 divisions of the North and the 12 divisions of the South, or Great Powers or Spirits or 24 Mysteries (in sub-divisions) of the Stellar Cult, and on "the Arms" of the Cross you will perceive the same 12 dots, the three parts of the arm showing 36 divisions, or sub-divisions, in "the Triangle," thus mixing the 36 divisions of Heaven of the Solar with the *Stellar* 24 or double 12.

I also produce here a copy of Plates 65 and 66 (Plate F) Vatican Codex B, showing the four Brothers of Horus as supporters of the Four Cardinal Points. It is portrayed in a different form, "Stellar," from the previous one, and their names and attributes are written in Glyphs underneath. They are represented here as supporting the Tree or Pillar or Pole of Heaven as Stellar.

Plate G (see Frontispiece), representing the Tableau des Bacab restored, shows the raised Tatt Cross, i.e. Tattu the Place established for ever, within a Square (Heaven), and the four "Bacabs," with their Consorts placed at the Four Cardinal Points, as supporters, or Guardians of Heaven. This plate represents the Solar Cult, although much

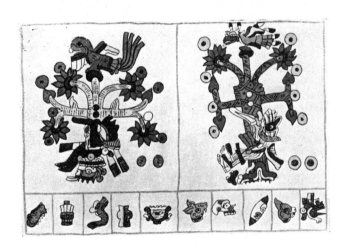

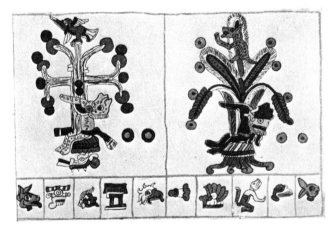

PLATE F.

The Four Brothers of Horus. (*From the Vatican Codex.*)

To face p. 244.

of the Stellar has been brought on and mixed with it ; even the names of the Bacabs (Maya) are written in the old Toltec Stellar Glyphs above them. The two central figures sitting one on each side of the Tatt Cross represent Horus in two forms, Earthly, and Spiritual ; although they have retained here one of the Signs and Symbols for his Stellar name, as shown on the left and portrayed by the head of the Crocodile, where we also see the Glyphs which denote that it is Horus, or the " Brow of the God Iu," the bringer or giver of life by water and food.

In another form the Tatt Cross consisted of a pedestal with four circular horizontal bars or shelves, constituting a kind of Altar-Cross. The name signifies " to establish," and is the Symbol of Stability as the fourfold foundation of the world, or an order of things, that was established upon the four quarters. The Tatt-Altar or Pedestal is the equivalent of the mount of the four Corners, or the Tree with four branches, or the Cross with four arms. It is the special type of Ptah, the establisher of the four Corners in the Solar Mythos ; but it existed as a Lunar Emblem for the Moon-God before the Solar and, as we see here, before that, in the Stellar as—" I am Tatt, the Son of Tatt, conceived in Tatt, and born in Tatt " (Ritual, ch. 1). Tatt was set up in Tattu, the established, or eternal region, the Station of the

Seven Great Gods in the Polar Region and first in the Stellar Cult.

This Tatt Pillar here represents the two Pillars of Tatt combined into one with the Cross added, and the Glyphs around tell you the same as the old Egyptian and the present-day Christian doctrines, i.e. through the raising of the Cross and the resurrection, or second advent, of Horus in Spirit form under the name of Amsu, he had established for ever Heaven as a Square for all his followers.

Although this plate (G) represents Solar Cult, it proves that the Mayas brought on many of their old Stellar Cult Signs and Symbols and embodied them into the New Cult, which they had just received from Egypt direct. (I find that the Peruvians (Incas) did the same in South America.) In Egypt they had destroyed all they could of the old Stellar and substituted the Solar, but in these far-off countries the pressure of destruction would not be so great, and the recent influx of the Solar Cult people would only be too pleased to have the Stellar Cult people amalgamate with them at the expense of retaining some of the old Signs and Symbols, which they probably quite understood. As did Moses when he lifted up the Serpent in the wilderness—to propitiate the followers of the Stellar Cult.

I also reproduce a copy of Plate 43, Borgian

Codex, showing these four Brothers or Attributes of Horus in still a different form (Fig. 83). The twelve ◯ represent the Twelve Stellar Powers.

The Four Brothers of Horus.

FIG. 83.—Copy of Plate 43, Borgian Codex.

Here again we see the Solar Symbol in the centre of the plate, proving how the Solar people brought on the old Stellar and made use of these Signs and Symbols. This picture represents and portrays

most graphically, one of the Egyptian stories of the
Creation, the decipherment of which it is not
necessary to give here.

FIG. 84.—Calendar Wheel from Duran.

Again, in this so-called Calendar wheel from
Duran (Fig. 84), which, in fact, is a Swastika Cross
representing the four quarters, or divisions of
Heaven, we have the names of the four Brothers,

or Children of Horus, in "*Zootype form*," one on each arm with the Symbol of the Solar Mythos in the centre, which shows a later innovation from the original. The four Winds as spoken of in

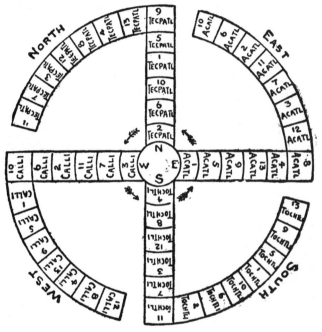

FIG. 85.—Mexican Calendar.

Revelation are here symbolized—one at each corner.

The Solar Cult symbol in its centre proves that this was brought on from the Stellar and appropriated by the Solar Cult people here in Central America.

I reproduce (Fig. 85) from the so-called Mexican Calendar the same kind of Swastika Cross representing the four quarters, or divisions of Heaven, and the names of the four Brothers, or Children

FIG. 86.

of Horus, as supporters *written* on the arms of the Cross, in Mexican.

These two Swastika Crosses are very important for this reason—on one we find the names written in Mexican, and on the other the same names in "Zootype" form, which gives the key to the Signs and Symbols, and enables us to read the other pictures correctly.

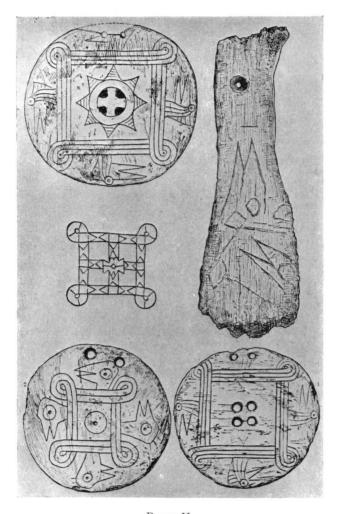

PLATE H.

Signs and Symbols of Horus on Engraved Shells from Mounds.

To face p. 250.

These are the Signs and Symbols, or Ideographic Glyphs (Fig. 86), in the Old Toltec of the names of the four Brothers of Horus, the Guardians or Supporters of the Four Cardinal Points which have been brought on from the old Stellar Cult and used in the Solar by the Mayas, as is proved by their portrayal in the above Bacab Tableau.

We also see (Plate H) from the plate of engraved Shells from mounds ("Maya and Mexican Manuscripts," p. 62, Fig. 10) these four Brothers represented by four Birds'-heads. In the upper one we have Paradise or Heaven represented as a Square, in the Centre of which there is an Eight-pointed Star = Heaven in eight divisions ; also in the centre of the Star is the Ideographic Symbol for Horus as Amsu, thus showing that he is the chief of the Seven Great Powers, or ruler as the eighth. The four Brothers or Children of Horus are depicted as four Birds'-heads, one supporting each quarter.

In the centre of the lower left we have a circle with the dot, equal to the Star at the summit of the Cone, a Sign and Symbol of Horus, God of the North and South, and in the centre of the lower right we have Heaven again as a Square with the four $\begin{smallmatrix} O & O \\ O & O \end{smallmatrix}$ = God of the four Quarters. In each case we have also the Birds'-heads as supporters and protectors of Heaven.

In the central figure we have Heaven divided

into four quarters with a Glyph—Ideographic name of Horus. This figure, however, is a much later representation, and those that formed it must have lost much of the original symbolism.

I think what I have here written and shown is sufficient proof of my contention as to the origin, interpretation, and importance attached to the Four Cardinal Points. The majority of our Brotherhood can only read the "Marchen," but if they wish for the truth they must go back and find the origin of "these Myths," to Old Egypt. Nowhere else can they find the explanation.

The above, I hope, will evince to the Brotherhood that although we make direct usage in our ceremonies of the Four Cardinal Points, and although they have hitherto lost the reason for so doing, I have now restored it to them. It will prove that there is a good authority for doing so, one far deeper and more abstruse than most of them imagined, brought on from the Old Stellar Cult Brothers.

Whatever incredulity some may feel, or scepticism expressed by others, remember we must instigate faithful introspection of these hidden mysteries if we wish for veracity, honesty, and fidelity, i.e. systematic coherence, and these points have been my aim. I write for the good and information of the Brotherhood throughout the world, endeavouring to inculcate what Freemasonry was and really is. Is there a Freemason living who can say why, when taking part in our beautiful ceremonies, he has a feeling rising within him which no ceremony in any church can arouse or still in the same way? At the time he " feels " a better man, and drawn to the Brotherhood and the Divine Creator differently from anything outside the Lodge. Outside the Lodge his faculties could not be elevated to the same standard. Can any brother answer why? I doubt it, except he knows and understands the " hidden mysteries " of the past. Then he will answer, because Freemasonry is the truest religion in the world, which has been brought on for countless ages by the Brotherhood, Pure and Unsullied. Let us seek the Truth, Brothers, and when found *I can assure* you *that it will not " shake your faith " whatever religious Cult you may follow outside the Lodge*, but on the contrary it will give you full knowledge of the truth, past and present, which will be a guide to you for the future, strengthening your belief and faith in Freemasonry as the One Great Original Religion of the World, and will give you the certainty of knowing which part of the Eschatology you are following as your religious belief outside the Lodge, because all the religions of the world have their origin in one or other part or parts of the Mysteries, or Eschatology of the Ancient Egyptians, and all

your supposed chronological dates in the V.S.L.
you will have to alter, not as a revolution but
from knowledge of evolution eventually determin-
able by you all.

XII

OPERATIVE MASONS

It has hitherto been a great question of discussion which is the oldest, the Operative or Speculative, and whether one was derived from the other or not. So far, no one has ever pointed out the origin of Operative Masons, and the relation of the one to the other.

The officers of the Operative Lodge "Mount Bardon," and the Operative Society, have been kind enough to furnish me with much of their Ritual, Signs and Symbols, and their interpretation of the same, and have suggested that I should give some explanation of the Operatives, as so many Speculative Brothers are interested in them.

I am glad to have the opportunity of doing this, and to show here some of the differences between the Operative and Speculative. I would, however, strongly impress upon my readers that the question, "does the Operative know more than the Speculative," or "the Speculative know more than the Operative," is futile, because they are each different. There cannot be any comparison drawn. The whole of the Operative working is the first and second Mysteries only out of the seven —later twelve—of the old Stellar Cult people, with some innovations from the Solar Cult. The explanations and uses of the ancient Signs and Symbols given to them was *for Operative work alone*.

The Speculative is the Ritual and Eschatological rendering of these seven, and later twelve, Mysteries in the Stellar, and all the Mysteries in the Solar, the latter being a continuation of the former, as the result of progressive evolution of thought to a higher degree.

The orientation of the Speculative Temples was originally South, then North, and finally East ; they corresponded to the changes from the primary god Set at the South Pole to Horus at the North Pole, and then finally changing from North to East in the form of Atum-Iu. With the Operatives their primary orientation for Temples must have been South first and then changed to the North, because their word " El Shaddai " signifies Set, God of the South and not the North, although they still carry on this name as God of the North Pole Star. This is not correct. It should be Horus-Khuti, or Horus Behutet, or Horus Anup.

The Operatives have changed their position from North to East in working their ceremonies the same as the Speculatives, but this is a Solar inno-vation. The Supreme Masters' position should still be North with them, as they are Stellar Cult, and working or Operative Masons, and had nothing to do with the Eschatological side originally, although I find some of it in their present Ritual, which must have been introduced during the Solar Cult. This I will show a little later by the Symbols they use and their present explanation of them.

I have already mentioned (*supra*) that the Operative Masons first came into existence at the time when the first old priests built their Temples, that these builders of Temples were the " Ari " of the seventeenth Nome of Upper Egypt, and in Egyptian were called " Craftsmen and Com-panions," and that they were initiated into the first and second Mysteries only. *The Sacred Signs and Symbols were given them as a guide to know-ledge, how to form and build with various angles, circles and other figures, by which the Architect could, by crossing and placing in various positions, portray for their guidance the buildings for the old High Priests.* They were initiated into the first and second Mysteries so that they should keep the secrets of these old buildings. The first Temple was that built at Edfu, and no builders were ever allowed to attend to these matters but those of the " Ari " in Egypt. They were all naked at first, except a small piece of bark cloth

18

in front, in the form of a triangle. These Operatives included all kinds of workmen required to build these Temples—Blacksmiths, Masons, Carpenters, etc. Remnants of these still exist at the present day in Africa, the Kaverondo Blacksmiths, who possess all the old secrets.

Whenever an exodus of these old Stellar Cult people from Egypt took place, they were accompanied by a full complement of these old builders, or Operatives, as well as by a priest. These priests possessed all the secrets of the mathematical and geometrical figures that could be constructed out of, or by placing together, their Sacred Signs and Symbols in various ways, as well as the Eschatological explanation of the same. That is the reason we find all the old Temples in Africa, Europe, Asia, Central and South America were built on the same plans during the Stellar Cult. During the Solar these were changed, and that probably accounts for some of the Solar Symbols now used by these old Stellar Cult Masons ; but although they have some of the Solar Cult Symbols, they still use a Stellar application, or definition, as far as they can to them.

The frieze of the Temple of Xochicales in Mexico is a good and typical example of a Stellar Cult building with Iconographic carvings, etc., well portrayed. (The reason for these Iconographic depictions was that in the Stellar Cult the Great

God and all his attributes were portrayed in Zootype form, whereas in the Solar these were depicted in the Human form, which type had not come into existence during the time of the Stellar Cult.)

The characteristic Solar Cult buildings are well portrayed and may still be seen at Mitla, Oaxaca ; on these we never find any Iconographic figures— but sometimes find human depictions. I mention these two as good examples still extant, but numerous remains of all Temples of both Cults are found in Central and South America and some in Africa.

They bonded the corners in Solar Cult, and at the latter part built arches, but these did not come into existence until the Fourth Dynasty. Hence we never find an arch during the Stellar Cult period, but only lintels.

The old Operative Masons show by the Triangle and the Swastika how they discovered the art to build arches. The first by the overlapping of the sides of the Triangle of Set and Horus, and later by converting the square of the Swastika into the Circle. (For the origin and meaning of the Swastika, see *supra*.)

Space does not permit me to give or to explain all their signs and symbols, and their uses as Operatives, but I will give a few as examples, which I trust will make it quite clear both to the

Operative and Speculative Mason, that the two classes were always two classes—*the one workers in Material, the other workers in Spiritual form.*

In Fig. 87 we have the triangles of Set and

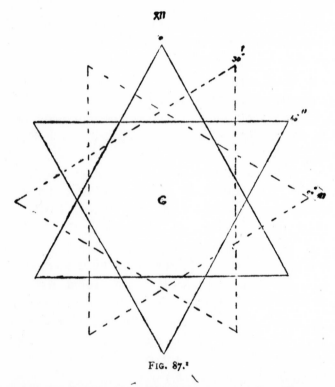

FIG. 87.[1]

Horus with Consorts added as a symbol of Heaven in twelve sub-divisions (see " Signs and Symbols of Primordial Man "). Fig. 88 is the same, with the angles for the Architect and builders to work on.

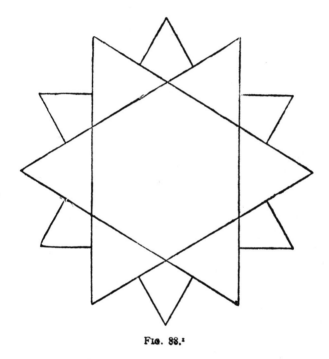

Fig. 88.[1]

---

[1] These figures are pairs, and their combinations may be seen by tracing one on paper and placing it over the other.

Fig. 89 is another symbol or division of Heaven in twelve divisions, and Fig. 90 is formed out of this for the builder.

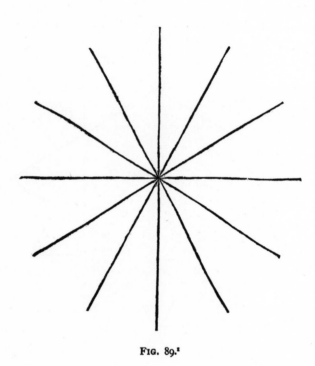

FIG. 89.[1]

FIG. 90.[1]

Fig. 91 is another form of Heaven in twelve subdivisions formed by the triangles of Set and Horus, with Consorts added. Fig. 92 shows how the builder can vary this angular form into part circular, still retaining the bases of the original.

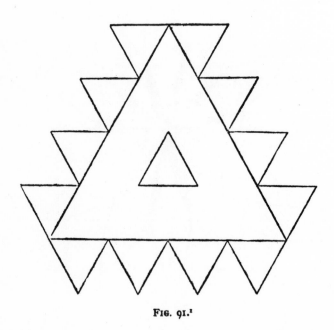

Fig. 91.[1]

[1] These figures are pairs, and their combinations may be seen by tracing one on paper and placing it over the other.

FIG. 92.[1]

In Fig. 93 we have the triangle of Set and Horus (North Horus, South Set), with the two at the equinox, East and West, which Shu added to that of Horus, forming four divisions of Heaven and their four Consorts added, making the Heaven

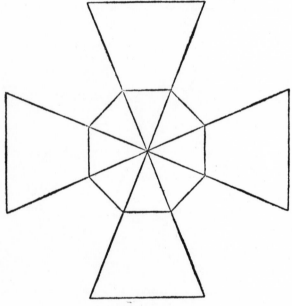

FIG. 93.[1]

in eight divisions. Depicted in Fig. 94 in another form, to give the Architect of the buildings different forms and angles by the crossing of the same two figures. This is a sign and symbol for Heaven in eight divisions, Stellar Cult, symbolizing the

Am-Khemen, the paradise of the eight Gods—that is,
of Anubis or Horus, and the seven Glorious ones.

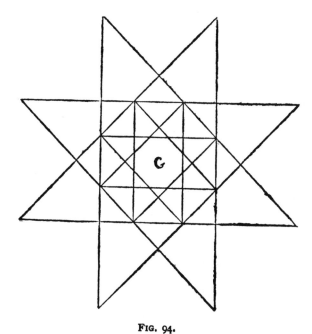

FIG. 94.

¹ These figures are pairs, and their combinations may be seen
by tracing one on paper and placing it over the other.

Another combination is formed by Figs. 95 and 96, the interpretation being the same.

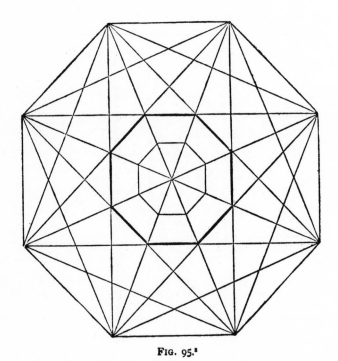

FIG. 95.[1]

---

[1] These figures are pairs, and their combinations may be seen by tracing one on paper and placing it over the other.

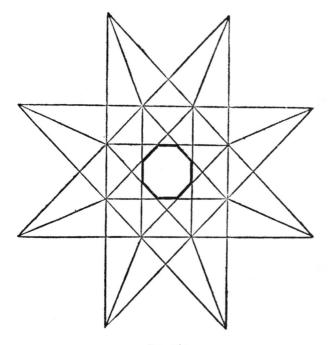

FIG. 96.¹

Figures 97 and 98—the two triangles of Horus and Set in a different variation—show how to make pentagon-shaped figures. Fig. 97 is the Egyptian symbol called *Sb aau*, the abode of Stars, or subdivision of the Celestial world-paradise, being formed by the triangles of Set and Horus (see *supra*). The landmark here should point to the North Star.

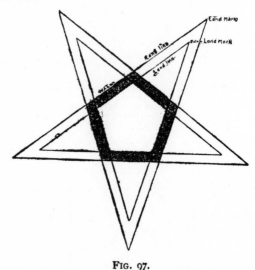

FIG. 97.

These figures show how the Operatives form a perfect Pentagon. It shows Heaven in the form and shape of a Pentagon. I am of opinion that for a short time at least, this was one form of our Lodges or Temples, and I make this statement for the reason that in the East the Lodge and Altar are

occasionally found as a Pentagon ; but if it were
so it did not last long, nor was it widely distributed.

FIG. 98.

Fig. 99 shows how the Operatives make the circles from these triangles.

FIG. 99.

Fig. 100 is the triangle of the Operatives—each side representing symbolically one of the three masters, or grand originals, or trinity—Horus, Shu, and Set. Fig. 101 is the same, showing the Architect and builder how he can vary the straight lines to curves and yet keep the same fit for the builders.

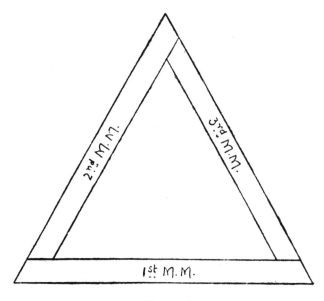

FIG. 100.[1]

---

[1] Figs. 100 and 101 are pairs, and their combinations may be seen by tracing one on paper and placing it over the other.

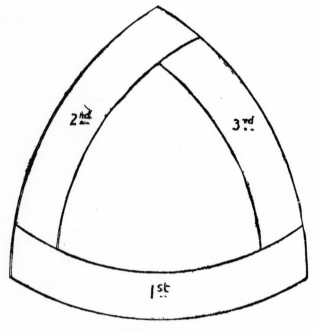

FIG. 101.[1]

In Fig. 102 we have the triangle of Set modified with plumb-line from the Pole Star down to the centre of the Earth, which gives the builder a square angle, level, and plumb rule all in one (see Ritual). You can prove if a Temple underground has its roof true to the upright wall. All Masters in the Operative 8th degree have it.

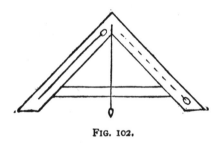

FIG. 102.

Fig. 103 shows the division of Heaven into two squares, or Heaven as one square and Earth as another ; also it shows the division into eight parts, the one square being superimposed upon the other, and Fig. 104 shows Heaven in eight divisions, Am-Khemen, the paradise of the Eight Gods, i.e.

Anup and the seven Glorious ones. The combination of the various triangles shows how the two squares can be formed, or, vice versa, the triangles out of the two squares.   There is much that could be

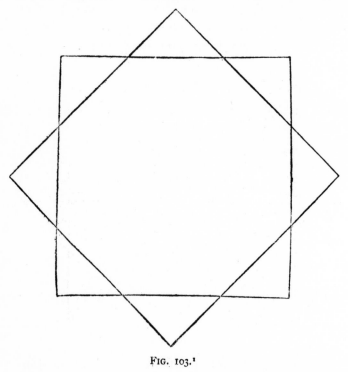

FIG. 103.[1]

written on these figures regarding the ancient Esoteric doctrines.

[1] These figures are pairs, and their combinations may be seen by tracing one on paper and placing it over the other.

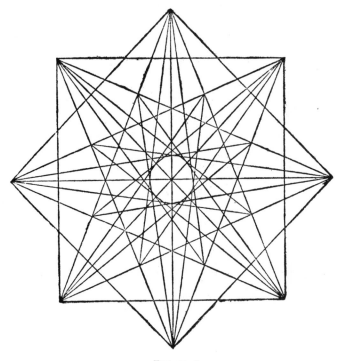

FIG. 104.[1]

Fig. 105 represents Heaven in twelve divisions, and Fig. 106 plans from these triangles for the builders and masons to work from.[1]

FIG. 105.[2]

[1] These figures are pairs, and their combinations may be seen by tracing one on paper and placing it over the other.

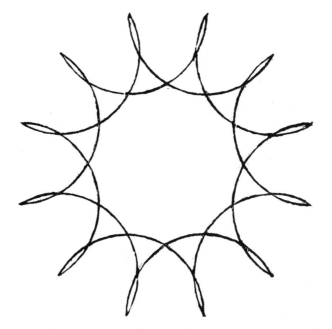

FIG. 106.[1]

Fig. 107. These two symbols or designs are very ancient, and were formed by the Master Architect from the triangle of Horus, God of the North, and the symbol for the Celestial Paradise of the North. If our Operative Brothers do not understand how to set out these, or if they have

FIG. 107.

" Both these designs are handed down to us [Operative Masons] in England. We have sent them to India and China, and the Operative Lodges reply that they have them, and that they are on some of their oldest Temples."

lost the secret of setting out these from the triangle of Horus, I shall be pleased to show them—at present they do not do it, yet it is one of the oldest and most secret and sacred symbols.

Fig. 108 represents the seven Pole Stars—the seven Glorious ones—circling around the one G—T.G.A.O.T.U.—i.e. Heaven in seven divisions (see " Signs and Symbols of Primordial Man "). Fig. 109 represents various angles, circles, and figures which can be made out of this for the builder.

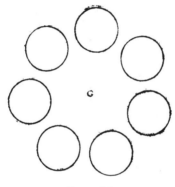

FIG. 108.[1]

---

[1] Figs. 108 and 109 are pairs, and their combinations may be seen by tracing one on paper and placing it over the other.

FIG. 109.[1]

Fig. 110 represents the same six Pole Stars with the one Central, or Heaven in seven divisions, —the seven circles of Ursa Minor—in different form for the builder to work on.

FIG. 110.

" Our Arch apprentice takes an OB. on this Sacred Seven."

" This gives the track for the feet when going round in the Arch degree."

Fig. 111. Here iii is the Ru (Egyptian An, see *supra*).

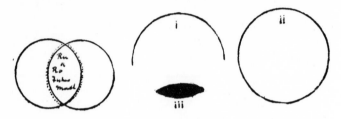

FIG. 111.

"*The root or key to our Operative Arch Masonry is the half-circl &*
the circle and the sign as fig. iii.   This figure iii is the unit that we
are to use to draw the Seven.   Give me the length of the unit simply
by two pinholes, and I will draw the figure without any pencil
or rule, simply a pair of compasses.   Fig. iii in the Operative
system refers to Life."   (See Speculative explanation *supra*.)

Fig. 112 is the Northern division of Heaven into twelve parts, (see "Signs and Symbols "). Heaven was divided into twelve divisions of the North, and twelve divisions of the South during Stellar Cult, and we have here the representation of the same.   These are the twelve divisions of Heaven, the twelve Camps of the Stellar Cult, the twelve Tribes of the Children of Israel, and various other twelves in many forms. Fig. 113 gives various angles and points for the information of the builder.

All the foregoing are of pure old Stellar Cult origin, and I will now give two of their Solar innovations.

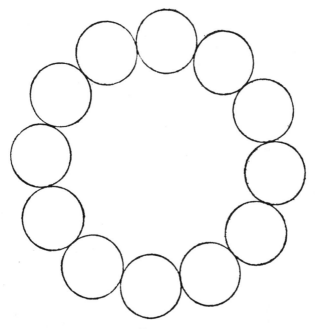

FIG. 112.[1]

"*The Operative Arch Masons require this to be all set out without being allowed to go to the centre. It is Holy ground within the twelve circles.*"

[1] Figs. 112 and 113 are pairs, and their combinations may be seen by tracing one on paper and placing it over the other.

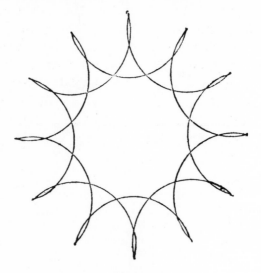

FIG. 113.

Fig. 114. This was part of the Solar Cult, and did not come into being until the Fourth Dynasty.

FIG. 114.

"This is how the Arch Masons teach their Candidates curved work. With left breast as centre strike out   . With right as centre strike out   . With neck as centre put in the invert."

Fig. 115. This symbol is the Swastika, and an •innovation brought on during the Solar Cult (see *supra*). The Stellar people formed a square originally with the two triangles of Set and Horus, and the formation of the heavens in the form of a square, or four quarters, was a later form and a Solar symbol. The Operatives have therefore formed out of this various figures,

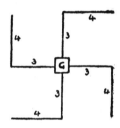

FIG. 115.

" This used by all right divisions."

both squares and circles, or a circle on four divisions, and learnt to build the true arch from this during the Fourth Dynasty.

But although the Operative Masons use now the Swastika in the form of the four divisions of Heaven, with the Four Brothers, or Children of Horus, as the representation of the Four Quarters and the Four Supports thereof, yet to

prove my contention that they were originally
Stellar Cult people, descendants of the old Ari of
the Seventeenth Nome of Upper Egypt, I will
give here another proof, namely, that they use the
" *original Stellar Cult Swastika* " in their ceremonies, which was in the form of Fig. 116—

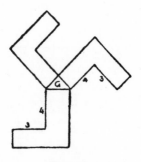

FIG. 116.

"This is used by the York division only."

and which we " Speculative " Masons do not use,
having lost the Eschatological signification, as well
as the old Sign and Symbol, but which I now
restore to them.

The interpretation and meaning of this Symbol
is as follows :—

1. There is the Triangle in the centre, representing Heaven in three divisions (G).

2. There are three arms which represent the three supports of Heaven, these representing the "Three Grand Originals" in the R.A.C. All R.A.M. will recognize this when the "Three meet to form the Triangle." Their position and action is one of "support," like on the "five points of Fellowship," "they meet and agree to support" the Triangle, a representative symbol of Heaven and T.G.G. of T.U., in the Stellar Cult.

3. The Primary Trinity is here represented as Horus, Set, and Shu.

4. These also represent the three primary Elemental Powers divinized—also the Three Seasons of the year, as ancient Egyptian—in the Stellar Cult (see *supra*).

5. This Sign and Symbol, although as old as the Stellar Cult, and Sacred Symbol still used by the "Operative Masons" of the York division only (for other reasons than here stated), has been brought on, and is at the present time used as a Totem Sign for the County of Kent and the Isle of Man. It is also found in many parts of the world under various phases. This "Swastika" of the Stellar Cult *is used by the York division of the Operative Masons only*, thus proving that their old Brother Operative Masons have preserved the true original, and have not contaminated their Ritual with the Solar innovation, which is not only very curious and instructive, but proves my

20

contention as regards the " Solar Swastika " being a Sign or Symbol not originally connected or belonging to them.

Fig. 117. As regards their statement " The present form of Speculative square is no good at all, as you will see "—this is not relevant to the

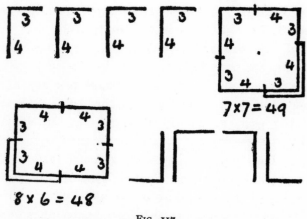

FIG. 117.

" The present form of Speculative Square is no good at all, as you will see." (Footnote communicated from Operatives.)

subject, as I have stated (*supra*). The one was for the builder, the other for Eschatology ; therefore each one is as good as the other for its purpose, as I would wish to point out to the Operatives —that in whatever form you find this Symbol, and there are many, the interpretation and meaning of the Ideograph is always the same, and could

not be varied to the Speculative Mason (see interpretation *supra*), whilst to the Operative the
various forms that this Symbol could be portrayed
in, meant much ; it gave him different angles,
squared the circle, or divided it into four divisions,
etc., so that comparisons between the Operative
and Speculative decipherment are futile. This was
a Solar symbol, and it is not found amongst the
old Stellar Cult remnants of the present time.

The Three Master Squares in the Operative
□ ☐ ☐ were formed on or out of the Triangle
in the centre of the above Swastika
embodied in the 47th Problem of
the First Book of Euclid (Fig.
118), and this Jewel is worn by
M.M. in Speculative who are
ignorant of its real origin and
meaning, which is that it is the
Triangle of Horus, the Three

FIG. 118.

Squares representing the Three Grand Originals
in one form, or the Primary Trinity.

Fig. 119. The Operative Arch Freemason wears
the Swastika as a Jewel with a Pole Star in its
centre. This proves how they have mixed up
this Solar symbol with their old Stellar Cult (explanation has been fully given *supra*). That the
Operatives have a varying number of arms to this
symbol further proves the innovation. This
symbol has *four arms only* in the Solar Cult.

The division into others has been caused by the Operatives placing one to seven, as the Power of the Pole, one to seven of the Glorious Ones, etc. These seven were represented in various forms— one was Horus, God of the North and afterwards God of the North and South ; two were Hu and Sa, attributes representing Spirit and Blood ; four were the four Brothers or Children of Horus, etc. (see " Signs and Symbols "), all powers or attributes of the one G.A.O.T.U., sometimes represented by

FIG. 119.

" The Arch Freemasons' Swastika is worn as a Jewel, and it is going with the Sun, the Pole Star being in the centre. Of course this is found on the top of the Arch Centre Altar. If the Arms are turned in the other direction it means death, Hell, and all evil. This drawing shows 4 Arms, but the Arch Masons have the same thing with 1, 2, 3, 4, 5, 6, and 7 Arms—corresponding to the degree."

" Cords," sometimes " Chains," and other forms, but all one and the same. But these had nothing to do with the Swastika, which was a Symbol of the four quarters, when Horus had changed from God of the Pole Star North in the Stellar Cult, to Atum-Iu in the early Solar.

These are the six circles of the Pole Star with G in centre (Horus). The Lines (six) represent the six powers represented by " ropes " as " men." (see Ritual of Ancient Egypt). *The top of this should be the North, not West, as it is Stellar Cult.*

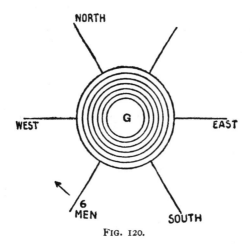

FIG. 120.

The Three Symbols or Marks of the three Operative Masons are—

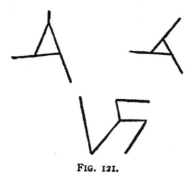

FIG. 121.

which are formed from the Primary Trinity in the Symbolism (1st) of the Three Triangles or the Triangle of Set and Horus with Shu added, and (2nd) the three Circles as—

FIG. 122.

These are very important, and if the reader will trace these out on two separate pieces of paper, and place one over the other, he will see how the triangle is unfolded into one centre triangle, with the three others around it. The Primary Trinity—the Three in One—the one ruling power.

I will give one more of the Operative Signs and Symbols, which is important because it shows the portrayal in the Stellar Cult of what we have also in the Solar under different symbols—"The Point within a Circle."

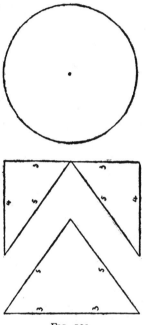

FIG. 123.

"This mark is found in Egypt, India, and many parts of the world. It is true to the 3, 4, 5 Angles, and the Operative teaching says it is a point within a circle—the root of the male and female system. The male portion is going with the sun, but the female is either standing still or going against the sun.

"There is an unwritten law in the Operative Craft that this sign is not to be explained to either Apprentice boys or to any but married Freemasons."

I reproduce the Operative explanation, which is quite sufficient to explain itself without my exposing any other secrets I ought not to.

The Operatives say that " Jabal " was their founder, but do not know how long ago he lived. This, I take it, is the Hebrew for Horus Behutet, and they can certainly claim that they have existed at least three hundred thousand years, because their Signs and Symbols, and the words " El Shaddai," prove that they were formed into the Brotherhood of " Companions and Craftsmen " at that time. Some of their present Ritual has been altered from the original, and passwords in Hebrew substituted for the original Egyptian, probably from the same causes as the Speculative. They salute the rising sun with the sevenfold salute which was originally Stellar, but brought on as an early Solar custom. The seven-time salute, however, was taken from the Stellar and carried on, but in their Red degree they still have the old Stellar custom, i.e. their form of an Arch lodge is a circle under the dome of heaven. They have the circular altar in the centre exactly under the plumb-line which comes down from the God of the Pole Star North. There are seven steps up to the altar, which they refer to the seven spirits or seven sciences. Thus they set out on the floor or ground six points ; six men are placed on each arm between the steps and point, and at the proper time these slowly revolve around the altar seven times. The circle here is a representation of the Celestial Paradise situated at the North. (For explanation of the Plumb-line see Ritual of Ancient Egypt.) The seven steps represent the seven Glorious Ones, or Great Attributes of T.G.A.O.T.U., and the circle of men (thirty-six in all) represents the procession of the Stars of the Little Bear, the number of times going round represents the number of the stars. The Circular Temple was in existence long before those of the double square ; it was in the circular form that Temples were first built by the early Stellar Cult people. Those in the form of a double square followed after. The orientation of these circular ones will always be to the South, which would prove that they were built at the time of Set or El Shaddai, God of the South Pole. Although at the present day they teach the " landmarks " and " land lines " on the ground, also the centre sun line and the whole system of " setting out " a Temple true to the sunrise, on the day after which the Temple is named they set out their foundations true to the sunrise on the day that the Hebrews came out of Egypt (supposed), and teach the Master the " five-point system " of setting out the Temple. Here we see a mixture of Solar and Stellar. " The five-point system " is the correct old Stellar. " The setting out true to the sunrise " is Solar, and came into existence when the orientation changed from North to East. This can be proved by examining the remains of all these old Temples, examples of which I have mentioned. The old ruins at Zimbabwe in Africa form a most excellent example of the remains of the old Stellar Cult builders, proving most conclusively the great knowledge of Geometry, Astronomy, and Mathematics which the Master builders possessed. The Iconographic figures found there prove, too, how far the Speculative had advanced in his evolution of "the doctrines of Final things."

I am much indebted to the Grand Council of the Operatives for forwarding me their diagram of the "Five Great Circles," showing the formation of a "curved-sided pentagon," which we Speculative Masons have lost (Figs. 124-128).

I reproduce here the diagrams. For the information of my Brothers I give the Egyptian explanation, and not the Operative interpretation. The curved pentagon here on the centre has the same explanation and meaning as the one made by the two triangles, as represented in the centre of the five-pointed star (straight-sided)—the subdivision of Heaven or Celestial World " Sb aau " (see p. 270).

The Five Great Circles represent the Five Great Spirits, or Attributes, or Guardians, of the same. In the Mexican we often see these represented by five Houses or five glyphs ; this is the origin of our five points of fellowship, as we demonstrate that part of our ceremonies, given only in each case to M.M. or higher degrees, both in O. and S. (F to F, K to K, H to H, B to B, H. O. B.), thus faithfully promising to guard the secrets

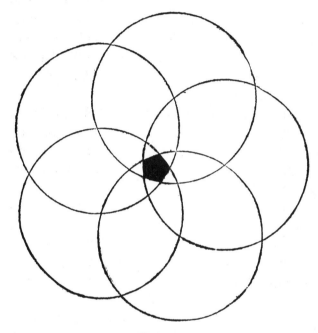

FIG. 124.

and to support our Brothers in the discharge of their duties.

These Five Great Circles represented a later phase in the evolution of Signs and Symbols than the five-pointed star, but both originated in the

Stellar Cult ; both the points and the circles represent, or are symbolical of, the Five Great Spirits

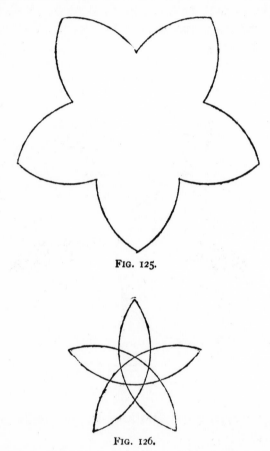

FIG. 125.

FIG. 126.

or Attributes, who guard the secret of Paradise, or
Heaven, and are supporters of each other, and in

the Operative sense, " Built on," or formed Heaven in the form of a pentagon, first with straight lines, secondly with curved sides—as the subdivision of the Celestial World, given to the Operatives by the Old Priests to show them the correct Mathe-

FIG. 127.

matical way to form the buildings, etc., in these forms, for their guidance and use.

The Sacred Sign " Ru " (Egyptian) which the Speculative Mason has lost, is still " formed " and used by the Operatives. It is formed by the two circles representing God of the North and God of the South (see Fig. 111), and was first formed when Horus became primary god. It represents the Saviour of the World who came by water, as the water of the inundation of the

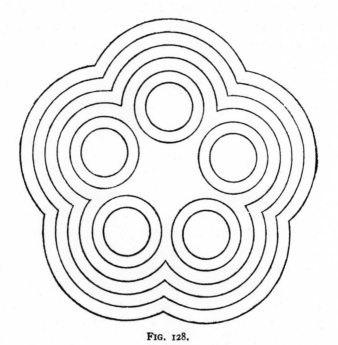

FIG. 128.

Nile, etc. (see *supra*). The Operatives use it in connection with the Five Great Circles, etc., which it is not necessary to explain here except that Eschatologically it is sixth great power, 5 + 1.

In the Operatives' form of death of H.A. they

take two planks 8 ft. long, 9 in. wide, fasten them
to the 60 by 20, or 3 to 1 Temple proportion.
They lay the body thereon, and tie hands and
feet and body thereto ; five men of equal height
lift the cross up until it rests on the " five points,"
or heads of the men under the centre and corners.
To the march of Israel,[1] they carry him seven times
round against the sun, all standing at the sign
of distress—

FIG. 129.

(but *this* is really not the ancient sign of distress ;
the meaning of this is quite another thing)—then
out of the Lodge, and the body is placed in the
tomb ordered for them by K.S.   This is only
done once a year, on the true day when H.A. was
slain (supposed).   To raise him on the five points
is to lift him and to carry him out flat on the
heads of five men.   We see a difference in the
Operative and Speculative here.   " His body being
laid crosswise " is an emblem of early Solar Ritual

[1] It was originally the March of the Priests of Memphis.
This is the only piece of music that has ever been found in
Ancient Egypt.   A copy of it came into my hands, and I
gave it to Ill. Bro. Capt. Rogan of the Coldstream Guards, who
orchestrated it for his band ; it is magnificent music.

and representation (see Swastika *supra*). The five men and the five points are Stellar, and refer to the death of Horus, the first which is associated with the five-pointed star (see my notes proving the tradition of the death of Osiris was brought on from the Stellar Horus). Of course in the Operative and Speculative the Hebrew version is retained, but the original was Horus, God of the North and South in Stellar Cult, and the Body should be on the Two Poles of North and South. I have discussed this in an earlier chapter (see Fig. 1, page 41). I do not wish any Brother to believe for one moment that because I have pointed out many innovations, made both in Operative and Speculative, I wish these Rituals to be altered in any way, because I do not ; we have used them now for some time, and all understand, or should understand, them. My writings are for the information of those Brothers who wish to know the origins of these things, and what they meant then.

I reproduce here an old plate of the Lodge and degrees of the Operative Masons, a Solar form. This is symbolic of a part of Amenta to the eighth pylon only, in which the first two mysteries were communicated to the Initiate—twenty-four pylons in all. The first mystery has been divided up into four degrees with these Operatives, " all of whom work with their hands." The second

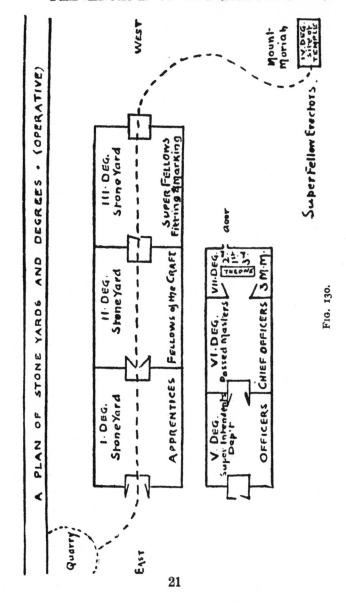

FIG. 130.

mystery has also been divided up into four degrees, "all of whom work with their heads or brains." In other words, you have here the working or Operative Lodge, based upon the Eschatological, with Esoteric rendering in working and building. All of the first four degrees here are working, and carry out the plans of the Architect, Mathematician, Geometrician, and Superintendent of the other four degrees. Thus you will understand my meaning when I have stated that these Operatives were initiated into the first and second Mysteries only. Their Lodge proves this, having only the representation of the eight pylons (see Ritual of Ancient Egypt). This form of their Lodge is Solar, and not the old Stellar form. I do not know if they have the old Stellar Lodge formation or not, but they will find it amongst the Mendozas at the present day. The orientation of the oldest Stellar Lodge was first South and then North ; when they changed to East they had adopted part of the Solar signs and symbols, and mixed them with the old Stellar, because it must be clearly understood that these old Operative Masons were constituted as such, by the Old Stellar Priests, and came into existence at the time of the early Stellar Cult. There is no trace in the Egyptian Ritual, or anywhere else, that I have been able to discover, of their being reconstructed again in the Solar, or any of the other

Cults. It is evident, however, that some Solar symbols were given them with the secrets of " setting them out " for their Architects and builders, by the Old Priests of the Solar Cult ; but there is no history of any further degrees having been conferred on them, and the fact that they have mixed up the Esoteric rendering of these Solar Symbols with that of the Stellar proves this.

In the " Arch-Masons Lodge " of the Operatives they place 12 Circles in a *round form* (see Fig. 112) *round the plumb-line down from the Pole Star;* on each circle they place a man. A *circular* Altar is placed in the centre, true to the plumb-line. The candidate is led 7 times round *outside* the circles, *then the man at the East moves*, which makes a door for the candidate to enter ; he is then led round 7 times *inside* the circle, and takes the Arch O. B. at the centre Altar. They say that the 12 men represent the 12 Tribes. The wall of living men represents 12 columns of Stone ; the men are human columns, or representatives of the originals. We see here that the Solar definition has been applied to a Stellar Representative. The 12 Circles represent the 12 divisions of Heaven, or the 12 Great Spirits of the North (there were also 12 of the South, see *supra*). The Altar being circular with the plumb-line from the Pole Star, proves it to be a Stellar portrayal, and the 7 times walking round represent the 7 Pole Stars or the

Khuti of the Egyptians. "*A man at the East moves*" also proves the Solar representative of a Stellar depiction. In the Egyptian it was "*a man at the North,*" which is the true representation before it "got mixed." The remains of 12 Circles of Stone N. (and 12 S.) are found in many countries at the present time (see *supra*).

When an Operative Lodge requires a new Chaplain, the Rev. Gentleman goes to a Lodge or degree of "Jachin"—*a Lodge of Priests*—and the *ceremony of initiation he has to undergo is unknown to the Operative members*. After his initiation, two Jachins conduct him to the Lodge door of the Operatives—in cap, gown, bands, and hood. He is brought in, and kneels while the prayer is given. The two Jachins lead him at once on to the square pavement, and he walks seven times round the central Altar and one of the Jachins puts the obligation to him. He is then taken to the Throne, and the 1st Master invests him with the Collar and Jewel, and tells him that he knows his duty so much better than the Master, and hands him the V. S. L. The Master gives him the grip and sign that will enable him to enter the Lodge at any time. He is then taken and installed in his seat on Mount Sinai in the S.E. corner. As Jachin represents God, he is saluted by all present in due form.

You will see by this he is not prepared as an

Apprentice ; he does not have a bond. The W.'s and D.'s and D.C. have nothing to do with the ceremony. *It is a religious and not a trade ceremony.* He does not go round on the border of the Carpet, but is taken at once to the " Square Pavement "—because it is for the High Priest to walk upon. He does not pay any fees to the Lodge funds, but he pays a fee to the Priests' or Jachins' Lodge. He has a special sign, which no other member of the Lodge dares to give. We see, therefore, here is critical proof of my contention on this point.

APPLICATION FORM.[1]

To the Superintendent of the Works of

THE WORSHIPFUL SOCIETY OF FREE MASONS

ROUGH MASONS, WALLERS, SLATERS, PAVIORS, PLASTERERS AND BRICKLAYERS.

I, ... being the Son of a Free Man and   years of age, humbly crave to be made an Apprentice to the Ancient and Honourable Craft.

I am prompted by a favourable opinion preconceived of the Fraternity and the desire for knowledge to enable me *to work at the Trade.*

I further promise and swear that I will conform to all the ancient usages and established customs of the Order.

WITNESS my hand this   day of   191

....

WITNESS

....

Proposed by :

Seconded by :

Supported by :

Proposed ....

Elected.................................

---

[1] A doctor's report is always required, and the medical examination of the candidate is that as for the Army, and he must be passed as " fit " or no application for membership will be granted.

NOTE.—You will see that the application for membership is *to work at the Trade*. This, you will perceive, is another proof of my contention as regards Operatives, and the distinction between them and the Speculatives.

To test a man by the triangle in the *blue* Lodge they have a frame as here shown :—

FIG. 131.

But to test a man in the arch or *red* Lodge the frame is curved, and the man goes through it.

FIG. 132.

You will find this cut in stone also as a design in church windows, etc.

In the 3rd degree the frames have 3 sides.
In the 4th degree the frames have 4 sides.
In the 5th degree the frames have 5 sides.
In the 6th degree the frames have 6 sides.
In the 7th degree the frames have 7 sides.

I trust what I have written will be sufficient to convince both Operative and Speculative Masons that there can be no question as to " which was first " or any other points which might cause any divisions. I have purposely not included the rituals of either, because these secrets of theirs should be kept ; they differ in a way, inasmuch as one is Operative and the other is Speculative, and it is quite possible during the later Christian times they might have mixed a little, but the two are distinctly different as stated.

I only trust that this very long chapter may render the position clearer to each Operative and Speculative Brother, so that no future question could arise to cause any division or unbrotherly feelings. I only write for the information and good of all Brothers of whatever clime or creed, in the name of T.G.A.O.T.U.

THE WORSHIPFUL SOCIETY OF THE FREE MASONS OF THE CITY OF YORK AND DIVISION.

OATH OF NIMROD.

Apprentice Degree (1st).

I, ... do, in the presence of
El Shaddai and of this Worshipful Assembly of Free Masons,
Rough Masons, Wallers, Slaters, Paviors, Plaisterers and Brick-
layers, promise and declare that I will not at any time hereafter,
by any act or circumstance whatsoever, directly or indirectly,
write, print, cut, mark, publish, discover, reveal, or make known,
any part or parts of the Trade secrets, priviledges, or counsells
of the Worshipful Fraternity or Fellowship of Free Masonry,
which I may have known at any time, or at any time hereafter
shall be made known unto me.

The penalty for breaking this great oath shall be the loss of
my life.

That I shall be branded with the mark of the Traitor and
slain according to ancient custom by being throtalled, that my
body shall be buried in the rough sands of the sea a cable's
length from the shore where the tide regularily ebbs and flows
twice in the twenty-four hours, so that my soul shall have no rest
by night or by day—

(Candidate signs the O.B.)

Given under my hand and sealed with my lips, this
day of   1913.

So help me El Shaddai and the holy contents of this book.

———

The First Master Mason—Take good heed to keep it right
well, for it is perilous and great danger for a man to forswear
himself upon the Holy Book.

NOTE.—We see here that the obligation refers
to *trade secrets,* and must therefore be of recent
origin. To prove this one only has to refer to the

later part of it, where " *his body is buried in the rough sands of the sea*." Now originally that could not enter into the obligation (in fact it did not in Egypt), because at Edfu, and in the 17th Nome, there was no sea, and probably the oldest brothers did not know much about the sea ; and it could not refer either to the Mediterranean, because that has, practically speaking, *no ebb and flow of tide;* and therefore this is a recent substitute for the old original Egyptian—which, I may add, is still extant, and which they have lost.

OPERATIVE MASONRY

THE OLD OPERATIVE OPENING AS IT WAS IN 1620, AND UP TO THE PRESENT TIME.

THE WORSHIPFUL SOCIETY OF FREE MASONS, ROUGH MASONS, WALLERS, SLATERS, PAVIORS, PLASTERERS, AND BRICKLAYERS.

To open the Lodge in the First Degree.

1st Master Mason—Brother Second Master Mason, is it your pleasure that we open the Lodge in the First Degree?

2nd M.M.—It is.

1st M.M.—Brother Third Master Mason, is it your pleasure that we open the Lodge in the First Degree?

3rd M.M.—It is.

1st M.M.—Brethren, assist us to open the Lodge in the First Degree.

1st M.M.—Brother Inside Guard, what is the first care of every Free Mason?

Inside Guard—To see that the Lodge is properly guarded.

1st M.M.—Brother Inside Guard, is the Lodge properly guarded?

Inside Guard—Worshipful Master Mason, it is.

1st M.M.—Brother Inside Guard, what is our next care?

Inside Guard—To see that none but Free Masons and Indentured Apprentices are present.

1st M.M.—To order as Indentured Apprentices.

1st M.M.—Brother Inside Guard, you will admit the Outside Guard.

1st M.M.—Brother Outside Guard, what is your position?

Outside Guard—Outside the door of the Lodge.

1st M.M.—Your duty?

O.G.—Being armed with a drawn sword, to keep off all cowans and intruders to Free Masonry, and to see that the candidates are properly prepared.

1st M.M.—Brother Inside Guard, what is your position?

Inside Guard—Within the door of the Lodge.

1st M.M.—Your duty?

I.G.—To admit Free Masons and Apprentices on proof, to receive the candidates in ancient form, and to obey commands.

1st M.M.—Brother Junior Warden's Deacon, what is your position?

J.W.D.—At the right of the Junior Warden.

1st M.M.—Your duty?

J.W.D.—To carry all messages and communications from the Junior Warden to the Senior Warden, and to await the return of the Senior Warden's Deacon.

1st M.M.—Brother Senior Warden's Deacon, what is your position?

S.W.D.—At the right of the Senior Warden.

1st M.M.—Your duty?

S.W.D.—To carry all messages and communications from the Senior Warden to the Deputy Master Mason, and to await the Master Mason's commands.

1st M.M.—Brother Master Mason's Deacon, what is your position?

M.M.D.—At or near the right of the Deputy Master Mason.

1st M.M.—Your duty?

M.M.D.—To carry all commands of the Master Masons from the Deputy Master Mason to the Senior Warden, and to see the same punctually obeyed.

1st M.M.—Brother Junior Warden, what is your position?

J.W.—In the north.

1st M.M.—Why are you placed there?

J.W.—To see the sun at its meridian, to call the brethren from labour to refreshment, and from refreshment to labour at the proper hours.

1st M.M.—Brother Senior Warden, what is your position?

S.W.—In the east.

1st M.M.—Why are you placed there?

S.W.—To see the setting sun, to pay the Masons their wages and to see that the working plans are placed in the place of safety.

1st M.M.—Brother Deputy Master Mason, what is your position ?

D.M.M.—At your feet.

1st M.M.—What is your duty ?

D.M.M.—To lay out schemes, draw designs, and see the Master Masons' work properly executed, also to open, rule, and close the Lodge when so commanded by the Worshipful Master Masons.

1st M.M.—Brother Deputy Master Mason, what is the position of the Master Masons ?

D.M.M.—Upon the throne in the west.

1st M.M.—Why are they placed there ?

D.M.M.—To see the rising sun, to open the Lodge, and to see that the Brethren are employed and instructed in Free Masonry.

1st M.M.—The Lodge being properly formed, before we declare it open, Brother Jachin.

Jachin—Most Holy and Glorious El Shaddai, Thou Great Architect of Heaven and Earth, Who art the giver of all good gifts and graces ; and hast promised that where two or three are gathered together in Thy Name, Thou wilt be in the midst of them ; in Thy Name we assemble and meet together, most humbly beseeching Thee to bless us in all our undertakings, to give us Thy Holy Spirit, to enlighten our minds with wisdom and understanding of this our worshipful and worthy Craft of Free Mason, that we may know, and serve Thee aright, that all our doings may tend to Thy glory and the salvation of our souls. This we humbly beg in Thy Name, O El Shaddai.

All say—So mote it be.

All say—" In the Lord is all our trust."

1st M.M.—In the name of King Solomon we declare the Lodge open for work in the First Degree.

We see here that the *oldest Stellar Cult* God is still used by the Operatives—El Shaddai = Set, who was Primary God of the South, although now they have placed him at the north, which is quite wrong.

This opening ritual for the first degree and all other ceremonies are known as "Old York Ritual," and it includes the whole of the charges, documents, and secrets of *the Ancient Guild Free Masons, Operative.*

NOTES ON OPENING.

It will be observed that there are three Master Masons, and they can do nothing unless the three agree, representing the Primary Trinity of Horus, Set, and Shu.

The Deputy Master Mason rules when the three masters are not present.

There are three Deacons.

The chaplain is known as Jachin.

The Masters and Wardens sit in such a position that they can face and see the sun.

In the temple, King Solomon, it is said, sat in the west and faced the east. The Operative Masters still do the same, but that was not the original position. This innovation was introduced probably at the time of the commencement of the Solar Cult. The Operatives, as is seen and proven here, have mixed their original Stellar with the Solar.

Once a year, October 2nd, the Operative Free Masons change their Third Master Mason.